NUTRITION AND DIET RESEARCH PROGRESS

PURCHASING FOOD AWAY FROM HOME

DEMAND PATTERNS FOR FAST FOOD AND FULL-SERVICE

NUTRITION AND DIET RESEARCH PROGRESS

Additional books in this series can be found on Nova's website under the Series tab.

Additional e-books in this series can be found on Nova's website under the e-book tab.

NUTRITION AND DIET RESEARCH PROGRESS

PURCHASING FOOD AWAY FROM HOME

DEMAND PATTERNS FOR FAST FOOD AND FULL-SERVICE

REBECCA EVANS
EDITOR

nova publishers
New York

Library of Congress Cataloging-in-Publication Data

ISBN: 978-1-63483-728-6

Published by Nova Science Publishers, Inc. † New York

CONTENTS

PREFACE

Food away from home (FAFH) is an important part of a typical American's diet and continues to increase as a share of the food budget. Rising consumption of a particular kind of FAFH—fast food—has been blamed for American's expanding waistlines and poor diet quality. The study examined in this book uses data from the 2003-11 American Time Use Survey to examine the effects of time-use behaviors, prices, sociodemographic characteristics, labor force participation, and prices on fast-food purchasing patterns in the United States before and after the Great Recession. Because fast food accounts for a large share of U.S. food expenditures and calorie consumption, a better understanding of the motivation behind trends in fast-food purchasing behaviors may help inform policies designed to improve the diet quality of Americans. This research complements previous studies that used food expenditure and food intake data (but not time-use data) to analyze the effects of demographic characteristics, prices, and income on fast-food purchases and consumption. In addition, this book discusses consumer spending at full-service and fast food restaurants, and the affect this has on the foodservice industry.

In: Purchasing Food Away from Home
Editor: Rebecca Evans
ISBN: 978-1-63483-728-6

Chapter 1

THE ROLE OF TIME IN FAST-FOOD PURCHASING BEHAVIOR IN THE UNITED STATES*

Karen S. Hamrick and Abigail M. Okrent

ABSTRACT

Meals, snacks, and beverages purchased at fast-food restaurants account for an increasingly large share of a typical American's food budget and have been blamed for Americans' expanding waistlines and poor diet quality. This study uses data from the 2003-11 American Time Use Survey to examine the effects of time-use behaviors, prices, sociodemographic characteristics, labor force participation, and prices on fast-food purchasing patterns in the United States before and after the Great Recession. Fast-food purchasers spend less time sleeping, doing housework, eating and drinking, and watching television than nonpurchasers, and more time traveling from place to place. They also tend to have higher incomes and higher education levels. While the time that Americans spent eating out at all restaurants declined during and after the 2007-09 recession, the share of the population eating at fast-food restaurants on a given day stayed fairly constant, seemingly unaffected by the economic downturn, but the share for sit-down restaurants declined.

* This is an edited, reformatted and augmented version of Economic Research Report Number 178, issued by the U.S. Department of Agriculture, Economic Research Service, November 2014.

What Is the Issue?

Food away from home (FAFH) is an important part of a typical American's diet and continues to increase as a share of the food budget. Rising consumption of a particular kind of FAFH— fast food—has been blamed for American's expanding waistlines and poor diet quality. Previous studies have attributed this increase in purchases of fast foods to many factors, including budget and time constraints, demographic and health characteristics, and market-level forces, but no study has been able to rigorously address the effects of all of these variables on fast-food purchasing behavior. This study is the first to extensively examine the effects of time-use behaviors, prices, sociodemographic characteristics, labor force participation, and prices on fast-food purchasing patterns in the United States before and after the Great Recession. Because fast food accounts for a large share of U.S. food expenditures and calorie consumption, a better understanding of the motivation behind trends in fast-food purchasing behaviors may help inform policies designed to improve the diet quality of Americans. This research complements previous studies that used food expenditure and food intake data (but not time-use data) to analyze the effects of demographic characteristics, prices, and income on fast-food purchases and consumption.

What Did the Study Find?

Americans purchase fast food to save time. Those that purchase fast food on a given day spend less time eating and drinking as a primary (main) activity, sleeping, doing housework, and watching television than the average for the total population. The difference in sleep time is considerable—fast-food purchasers spent 23 fewer minutes sleeping on a given day over 2003-11 than the average for the total population. In addition to spending less time in primary eating and drinking, fast-food purchasers were more likely than the average person to report no primary eating/drinking on a given day. Fast-food purchasers spent about the same amount of time as others in "secondary" eating; that is, eating while engaged in another, primary activity. However, fast-food purchasers were more likely to eat while at work or while driving a vehicle than others. To the extent that eating quickly may not be ideal and that eating is done while one is engaged in activities that demand focus suggests that fast-food purchasers have different, and perhaps poorer, eating habits than others.

Effects of Employment

On a given day in 2003-11, those who were employed were more likely to purchase fast food than those not employed. And those who were employed but on their day off were even more likely to purchase fast food than those employed and on a workday or those not employed.

Effects of Household Characteristics

Consistent with findings in other studies, household composition, income, age, and education play an important role in fast-food purchasing behavior. Relative to married and unmarried couple households with no children, a single-person household had a higher probability of fast-food purchase by 1.4 percent on a given day in 2003-11. "Other" households with and without children, typically multigenerational households, had the same increased probability. Single-parent households, however, had an increase in the probability of fast-food purchase of 2.5 percent relative to married households. Married and unmarried couple households with children had the same probability of fast-food purchase as couple households without children. Households with higher incomes and households with higher education were also more likely than other households to purchase fast food.

Effects of the Great Recession and Time Spent Eating out

During and after the Great Recession, the overall time that Americans spent eating out declined, which was associated with a drop in the share of the population who ate at sit-down restaurants. However, the share of the population that purchased fast food on a given day stayed fairly constant during and after the 2007-09 recession, seemingly unaffected by the economic downturn, while those employed were even more likely to purchase fast food than before the recession. In particular, employed single parents were 3.9 percent more likely to purchase fast food than others pre-recession and 5.2

percent more likely during and after the recession—a large increase in fast-food purchase behavior.

For the total population, there were small but statistically significant changes in time-use patterns during and after the recession—less time spent in paid work and in travel, more time spent in meal preparation and in watching television. However, time-use patterns of fast-food purchasers stayed faily stable and exhibited less change than those of the total population.

How Was the Study Conducted?

The study used data on time use and demographic and other characteristics from the American Time Use Survey (ATUS). The ATUS is a continuous, nationally representative survey of time use by Americans that has been conducted by the U.S. Bureau of Labor Statistics since 2003. ATUS data enabled researchers to compare time-use patterns of those who purchased fast food with those of the total population and other subgroups. An advantage of using these data rather than food intake data (i.e., National Health and Nutrition Examination Survey) or expenditure data (i.e., Consumer Expenditure Survey) is that the ATUS provides detailed information on time use by Americans and offers a unique perspective on the relationships between fast-food purchasing behavior and time variables that have been previously unexplored in the literature. Information on secondary eating was derived from the 2006-08 ATUS Eating & Health Module.

Descriptive statistics on time and frequency of purchase were estimated for subpopulations (gender, employment status, and fast-food purchaser) between 2003 and 2011 and also before and after the onset of the Great Recession in December 2007. Researchers conducted multivariate analysis on the probability of fast-food purchase by household type (i.e., single person, single parent, couple no children, couple with children, other households no children, and other households with children).

Introduction

Meals, snacks, and beverages purchased at fast-food and sit-down restaurants have become a large and growing portion of a typical American's food budget. In 1929, food purchased for away-fromhome consumption constituted only 13.4 percent of the average U.S. household's food budget, while in 2012, this share was 43.1 percent (USDA-ERS, 2013). During the past decade, however, the growth in food-away-from-home (FAFH) expenditures by establishment type has been uneven. Expenditures at fast-food restaurants decreased from about 4 percent to 3 percent of the total budget for all goods and services for an average U.S. household between 1998 and 2010 but seemed to be unaffected by the Great Recession (December 2007-June 2009). On the other hand, the share of total expenditures for goods and services attributed to sit-down restaurant meals grew from 1998 until 2006 and fell just before the Great Recession (Okrent and Alston, 2012). While consumers have decreased expenditures on fast food, this segment of consumption still accounts for a relatively large and growing share of the calorie intake by Americans (Lin and Guthrie, 2012).

The calories consumed from fast-food and sit-down restaurants constitute nearly a third of the energy intake by adults in the United States, and study findings suggest that the nutritional quality of these foods is lower than foods purchased for at-home consumption (Lin and Guthrie, 2012). In addition, fast food has been found to contribute to obesity (Chou et al., 2004; Davis and Carpenter, 2009; Currie et al., 2010; Chen et al. 2013; Alviola et al., 2013). On the whole, this evidence suggests that consuming FAFH may lower dietary quality and increase body weight and that different types of FAFH may affect dietary quality and individual body weight differently. The linkage between food consumed at fast-food and sit-down restaurants and poor nutritional outcomes has led to Federal initiatives to promote consumption of healthier options and limit marketing and access of these foods to children (White House Task Force on Childhood Obesity, 2010). For example, in response to First Lady Michelle Obama's *Let's Move* campaign, several food companies, including McDonald's, pledged to limit the marketing of "unhealthy" products to children (Federal Trade Commission, 2012).

However, what if purchasing decisions at fast-food and sit-down restaurants are influenced not only by relative prices and marketing but by time constraints? In particular, Mincer (1963) argued that ignoring the value of time in demand relationships could produce biased results. In the new household economics, the value of time is an important factor affecting consumption, which suggests that households may substitute time-saving services for their own time (Becker, 1965).

Harms (2014) found that married women in the rural United States spent an average of 122 minutes cooking and an additional 68 minutes in meal cleanup on an average day in the 1920s. Zick and Stevens (2009) found that food preparation time for women declined from an average of 92 minutes a day in 1975 to 51 minutes in 2006; for men, food preparation time increased by only 3 minutes during the same period and still averaged under 20 minutes per day. The authors conclude that these are secular trends that persist after controlling for demographic, economic, and household changes that have taken place over the three decades. Hence, households with two wage earners may consume more time-saving goods and services than do households with full-time homemakers.

This is the first study to extensively examine the effects of time-use behaviors, prices, sociodemographic characteristics, labor force participation, and prices on fast-food purchasing patterns in the United States before and after the Great Recession using data from the 2003-11 American Time Use Survey (ATUS). The advantage of using ATUS data versus food intake or food expenditure data (e.g., National Health and Nutrition Examination Survey (NHANES) and Consumer Expenditure Survey, respectively) is that time-use data enable researchers to examine the relationship of time spent in work, household production, and leisure activities to fast-food purchasing decisions. In addition, time diaries are considered a neutral method of collecting data on time spent in various activities and are less subject to under- and overreporting than surveys that ask for estimates of time spent on specific activities (Robinson and Godbey, 1997, chapter 4; Robinson et al., 2011).

Because the data range from 2003 to 2011, we could also test the impact of the Great Recession on the probability of purchasing fast food. Specific research questions addressed in this study include the following: (1) What individual- and household-level characteristics, including how individuals spend time, are associated with fast-food purchases? and (2) Did fast-food purchasing behavior change over the recent business cycle? A better understanding of the motivation behind the trends in fast-food purchasing behaviors will help inform policy designed to improve the diet quality of Americans.

RELEVANT LITERATURE ON DETERMINANTS OF FAFH DEMAND

Demand for FAFH is typically modeled as being a function of prices and income—the standard utility maximization framework. With the exception of Okrent and Alston (2012) and Richards and Mancino (2013), most previous studies have modeled demand for FAFH as a composite good and have generally found demand for FAFH to be more responsive to price- and income-induced expenditure changes than food at home (FAH) (see Okrent and Alston (2011) for a review of these studies). Okrent and Alston (2012) found demand for fast foods to be almost perfectly inelastic to changes in prices (-0.13) and demand for meals from sit-down restaurants to be quite price elastic (-1.96). On the other hand, Richards and Mancino (2013) found the price elasticity of demand for meals at fast-food and various types of sit-down restaurants to be between -0.5 and -0.9. Demand for different types of FAFH—in particular, fast foods—may depend on time constraints and convenience, sociodemographic characteristics, and macroeconomic forces like the business cycle rather than just relative prices and income.

Becker (1965) developed the theory of time allocation, which accounted for the time input into the commodities and activities that a household produces via a household production function, as well as the time constraint faced by individual household members. The household's utility function contains the commodities and activities and is maximized subject to the two constraints. One household commodity is meals. An increase in the value of an individual's time would lead to a substitution toward goods. "For example, an increase in the value of a mother's time may induce her to enter the labour force and spend less time cooking by using pre-cooked foods...." (p. 514). Becker's theory of time allocation spawned an extensive literature on home production (see Gronau (1986) and Gronau (1997) for thorough literature reviews). Indeed, Gronau commented that the household production function highlights that "one cannot separate the analysis of consumption behavior from the analysis of time use" (1997, pg. 199).

In keeping with the Becker household production model, several studies have argued that increased consumption of meals and snacks at fast-food restaurants has largely been driven by opportunity cost of time within a typical American household (e.g., Davis, 2013). Most studies account for the opportunity cost of time by using wage, labor hours, women's labor force participation, presence of working spouse, and employment status to proxy for the time constraint faced by households making food purchasing decisions. With the exception of Huffman (2011), most of these studies use cross-sectional data and assume that prices faced by consumers in a particular period are constant. All of these studies also include sociodemographic variables, arguing that household size, age, race, and other characteristics are important determinants of FAFH consumption. More recently, studies have begun to analyze structural changes in food consumption (i.e., substitution out of FAFH and into FAH) due to the most recent recession.

Much of the research that investigates the impact of the time constraint on household production and demand for FAFH treats FAFH as a composite. These studies generally found that the value of time for a household manager (the household member responsible for meal preparation, including grocery shopping, cooking, baking, assembling, and serving food, and cleanup after the meal, sometimes assumed to be the female) has a positive effect on demand for total FAFH (Prochaska and Schrimper, 1973; Sexauer, 1979; Soberon-Ferrer and Dardis, 1991; Yen, 1993; Nayga and Capps, 1994; Byrne et al., 1996; and Dong et al., 2000). However, a few studies, namely Huffman (2011), Redman (1980), and Kinsey (1983), found the household time constraint to be a less important determinant of demand for FAFH. Kinsey (1983) argued that while this result may appear to contradict theory, household managers need not increase FAFH expenditures to substitute relatively inexpensive goods and services for time if the cost of purchasing certain types of FAFH (i.e., fast foods) is cheaper than food at conventional sit-down restaurants.

Several studies investigated whether the value of time has a differential effect on FAFH by establishment and meal type. McCracken and Brandt (1987) and Stewart et al. (2004) found that an increased value of the household food manager's time increased expenditures on fast food more than on meals from sit-down restaurants. Similarly, Byrne et al. (1998) and Stewart and Yen (2004) found the effect of household manager hours to have a positive impact on demand for fast foods but negative impact on demand for sit-down foods. Contrary to previous findings, Jekanowski et al. (2001) did not find any significant effect of this variable on per capita fast-food sales. Jensen and Yen (1996) examined the demand for FAFH by meal type—breakfast, lunch, and dinner—and found that the effects of wife's employment are positive on both the probability and level of expenditures on lunch and dinner as FAFH, but wife's employment did not seem to affect breakfast as FAFH.

Related to opportunity cost of time, the above studies also acknowledge that meal preparation, and, hence, demand for FAFH is also determined by household composition, including presence of children, family size, martial status, and gender of household heads (primary wage earners in the household). Prochaska and Schrimper (1973) and Soberon-Ferrer and Dardis (1991) found that even though the presence of children in the household negatively affected demand for total FAFH, the size of the household increased demand for total FAFH. The argument is that additional number of adults in the household lead to additional FAFH because of time constraints related to employment and social activities. Byrne et al. (1996) found household size had a negative effect on demand for total FAFH, arguing that there are economies of household size in meal preparation at home. Byrne et al. (1998) found that family size was only negatively related to expenditures at sit-down restaurants and positively related to expenditures at fast-food restaurants.

Later studies began investigating "nontraditional" households by including marital status in the analysis because of changes in traditional household structure (e.g., from married to single or multi-generational households). Byrne et al. (1998) found that unmarried households spent less on FAFH than married households regardless of restaurant type, arguing that fewer people were involved in the FAFH occasion. Contrary to this finding, Stewart and Yen (2004) and Stewart et al. (2004) found that single-person households spent around \$0.5-\$3.0 *more* per week at fast-food and sit-down restaurants than married households but single-parent households spent \$0.30-\$1.70 **less** than married households at both types of FAFH establishments.

Lastly, gender of the household manager also seems to affect demand for FAFH, but empirical evidence is mixed. Byrne et al. (1996) found that households with female household managers had lower expenditures than those with male household managers, which they attributed to males having less culinary skills than females. Byrne et al. (1998) found that female household managers who worked spent less at upscale and midscale sit-down restaurants but more at fast-food restaurants than male household managers.[1]

Only recently have extensive time-use data been applied to time allocation models to examine tradeoffs between time and market prices in meal preparation and consumption of prepared foods.

Hamermesh (2007) paired data from the 1985 Time Use Survey and ATUS with data from the Consumer Expenditure Survey for 1985 and 2003 to examine how married households combined expenditures on goods and time to prepare or purchase meals and snacks. Hamermesh found large decreases in the time inputs into eating over the period, where eating appears to be a relatively goods-intensive commodity. Using the 2005 ATUS, Tashiro (2009) found that more time in paid work resulted in less time preparing food at home for all respondents; that time spent in purchasing prepared food increases with time spent in leisure activities for Whites and Hispanics; that Blacks increase their time spent purchasing prepared food with increases in paid work time; and that purchases of prepared food tend to increase with a person's education level. Lastly, Van der Lippe et al. (2004) examined outsourcing of domestic tasks in the Netherlands and found that income was the most important determinant of a household's likelihood to outsource. In particular, Van der Lippe et al. found that dual-earning households who spent more time in the labor market were more likely to outsource—which includes purchasing takeout meals—and that takeout meals were strongly related to the presence of children in the household.

The last thread of literature that investigates the determinants of FAFH demand addresses how economic downturns and the business cycle affect demand for different types of foods. In the most recent literature, some researchers have begun to analyze the effects of the most recent recession (December 2007 to June 2009)[2] and recovery on time-use patterns food expenditures, and dietary intake. Using 2003-10 ATUS data and analyzing cross-State variation, Aguiar et al. (2013) found that the bulk of the foregone market work hours was spent in leisure, and 30 percent of this time was reallocated to nonmarket home production, which includes a 12-percent increase in hours spent in core home production (cooking, cleaning, and laundry). Beatty and Senauer (2012) documented that food spending shifted into FAH from FAFH over the 2007-09 recession and into the recovery and also noted that low-income households spent more time on food preparation. In addition, Todd (2014) found that dietary quality improved between 2005-06 and 2009-10, which could be partly attributable to a 127-calorie decline in daily energy intake from FAFH (of which a 53-calorie decline is from fast-food consumption). Looking at how labor force status—employment and unemployment—affects consumption, Dave and Kelly (2010) found that a higher risk of unemployment is associated with reduced consumption of fruits and vegetables and increased consumption of snacks and fast food.

The literature on the determinants of FAFH purchase behavior in the United States examines a number of competing hypotheses as to why demand for FAFH has grown, including market prices, income, opportunity cost of time, household composition and demographics, and macroeconomic shocks. However, none of these studies were able to simultaneously explore many of these competing hypotheses due to data limitations. This study uses data from the 2003-11 ATUS to directly analyze demand for FAFH by type (fast-food and sit-down restaurant) as a function of individual- and household-level time-constraining activities (time spent in work, personal care, meal preparation, and leisure activities over the day); demographic, labor force, and household characteristics; and market-level characteristics. Also, since these data cover the 2007-09 recession, the longest and deepest post-World War II U.S.

recession, the study addresses the effects of business cycle events on fast-food purchase behavior.

DATA AND DEFINITIONS

To identify various FAFH activities and estimate frequency and time duration, we used data from the pooled 2003-11 ATUS. Although these data do not indicate dollars spent or calories consumed on FAFH, they do draw from survey respondents' time diaries of activities, as well as provide extensive demographic and labor-force participation information, information on all members of the household, and some geographic information. This enables researchers to identify different FAFH behaviors in different subgroups. As discussed in the literature, other data sources exist that can be used to model demand for fast food; for example, food intake data from NHANES and food expenditure data from the Consumer Expenditure Survey have been used to look at the effects of fast-food consumption on diet quality and the effects of prices and expenditures on fast-food consumption. However, these data sets do not contain information on all of the ATUS respondents' activities, as there may be important tradeoffs in time use that affect fast-food purchasing behavior.

The U.S. Bureau of Labor Statistics' ATUS is a continuous survey that began in 2003. Survey interviews are conducted by the U.S. Census Bureau nearly every day of the year to allow for analysis of weekdays versus weekends, holidays, and seasonality. One individual age 15 or older from each sampled household is interviewed about his or her activities for the 24-hour period from 4 a.m. the day before the interview to 4 a.m. on the interview day.[3] Survey respondents are asked to identify their primary activity if they were engaged in more than one activity at a time. They are also asked to report where they were and whom they were with for most diary activities.

The pooled 2003-11 ATUS microdata files contain 124,517 completed interviews, yielding a total of 2,462,919 activities in the respondents' time diaries. ERS used the ATUS Respondent, Roster, Activity, Activity Summary, Who, ATUS-Current Population Survey, Replicate Weights, and Methodology Case files.[4] (See references for Web site links.)

Estimation procedures outlined in the ATUS User's Guide (U.S. Bureau of Labor Statistics, August 2012) were followed. All estimates presented were weighted to be nationally representative. Averages were calculated as the mean. Standard errors were calculated according to Section 7.5 of the ATUS

User's Guide, using the balanced repeated replication method and the ATUS Replicate Weights file. A 90-percent level of confidence was constructed around each estimate and used to determine statistical differences. All differences between estimates discussed in the text are statistically different at the 90-percent level unless indicated as otherwise. SAS 9.2 and Stata 12 were used for estimatation.

ERS used the ATUS time diaries to infer whether an individual made a fast-food/carryout purchase (hereafter referred to as fast food) or ate at a restaurant (or related venue). ATUS "where" codes denoted the respondent's location during an activity, and researchers used this information in conjunction with the sequence of events relating to a fast-food purchase. Generally, if an individual reported time to travel to a restaurant and purchase food, the food purchase was classified as fast food; if an individual reported time to travel to a restaurant, eat the food, and then pay for the food, this purchase was classified as sit down. Note that ATUS data do not indicate the type of food and/ or beverage purchased, so the purchase could have been just a cup of coffee, or the food could have been purchased at a convenience store rather than a restaurant. For a small number of respondents, researchers applied other rules to identify fast-food and sit-down purchases (see appendix for more details and a discussion of the limitations to identifying fast-food purchase).

DESCRIPTIVE STATISTICS

This section describes differences in fast-food and sit-down restaurant purchasing behavior between subpopulations and over time. Because of evidence that the Great Recession has had a lasting impact on FAFH purchasing behavior, the first subsection discusses differences in time spent eating and drinking, and engaging in other household activities, and fast-food and sit-down restaurant participation rates by gender and employment status. The second subsection analyzes changes in fast-food and sit-down participation rates over the business cycle. All estimates are weighted to be nationally representative, and a 90-percent level of confidence was used to determine whether estimates were statistically different between subpopulations.

Differences Among Gender, Employment Status, and Fast-Food Purchasing Groups

In 2003-11, on an average day, Americans age 18 and older spent 67.5 minutes engaged in primary eating and drinking (i.e., eating and drinking as an individual's main activity) (Figure 1; see appendix tables 1 and 2 for more detailed time-use estimates, participation rates, and distributions of eating behaviors). This total comprises 14.1 minutes eating out, mostly at sit-down restaurants, and 53.4 minutes eating elsewhere.[5] In addition, 19.5 percent of the population ate at a sit-down restaurant on an average day in 2003-11, and 13 percent purchased fast food or carryout food (Figure 2). Eating at a sit-down restaurant and purchasing fast food are not mutually exclusive, as 1.7 percent of Americans did both on an average day during the period (not shown). Only about one-third of those who purchased fast food reported eating at the restaurant (not shown).

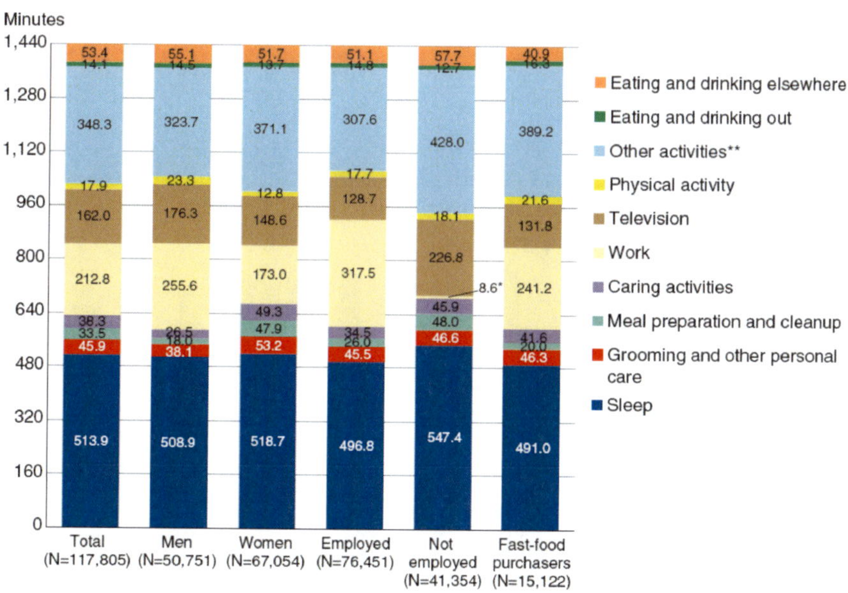

Notes: N = number of observations. *Time spent looking for employment is considered work. **Other activities includes all travel time.

Source: USDA, Economic Research Service estimates calculated from American Time Use Survey data.

Figure 1. Time spent in various activities on an average day, 2003-11, age 18 and older.

Time-use patterns of men and women over 2003-11 reveal many of the same differences identified by other ATUS researchers; in particular, men spend more time in eating/drinking activities, paid work, and watching television, whereas women spend more time in grooming; meal preparation, cleanup, and other household tasks; and caring for others. Interestingly, compared with women, more men ate at a sit-down restaurant (20.4 percent versus 18.5 percent) and purchased fast food (13.5 percent versus 12.5 percent). These findings are in line with Byrne et al. (1996), who argued that households with female household managers may purchase less FAFH because they have better cooking skills.

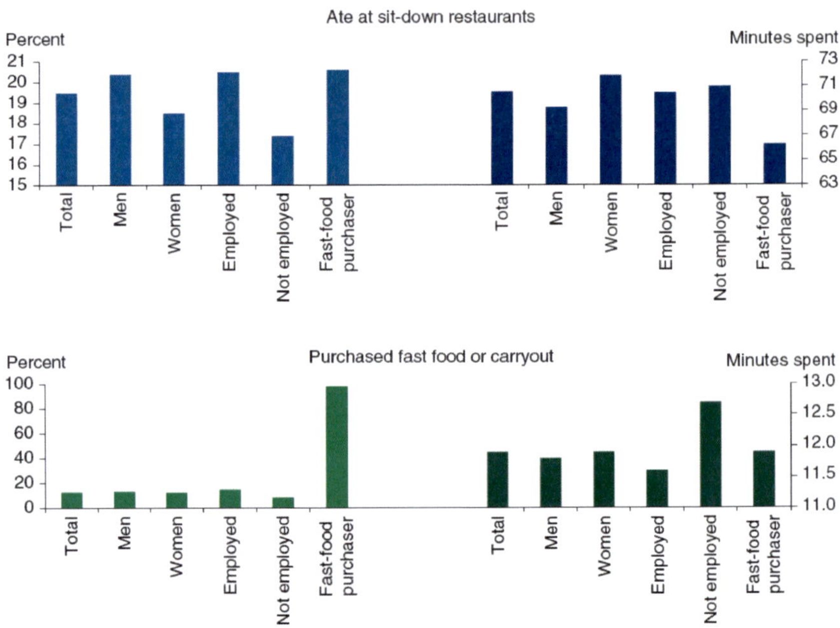

Note: Travel time is not included in the calculation of participation rates. FAFH = Food away from home.

Source: USDA, Economic Research Service estimates calculated from American Time Use Survey data.

Figure 2. Participation rates for FAFH, on an average day, 2003-11, age 18 and older.

The population that was not employed spent 8.6 minutes per person on an average day looking for work, which is considered a work-related activity. Because the ATUS data span the 7-day week, including holidays, and most people work only 5 days a week, employed averages reflect both those who are employed and engaged in paid work on an average day and those who are employed but did not engage in paid work. Those who were employed spent, on average, less time in eating/drinking than those not employed (65.9 minutes versus 70.5 minutes) and also less time in meal preparation and cleanup (26 minutes versus 48 minutes), on the average day.

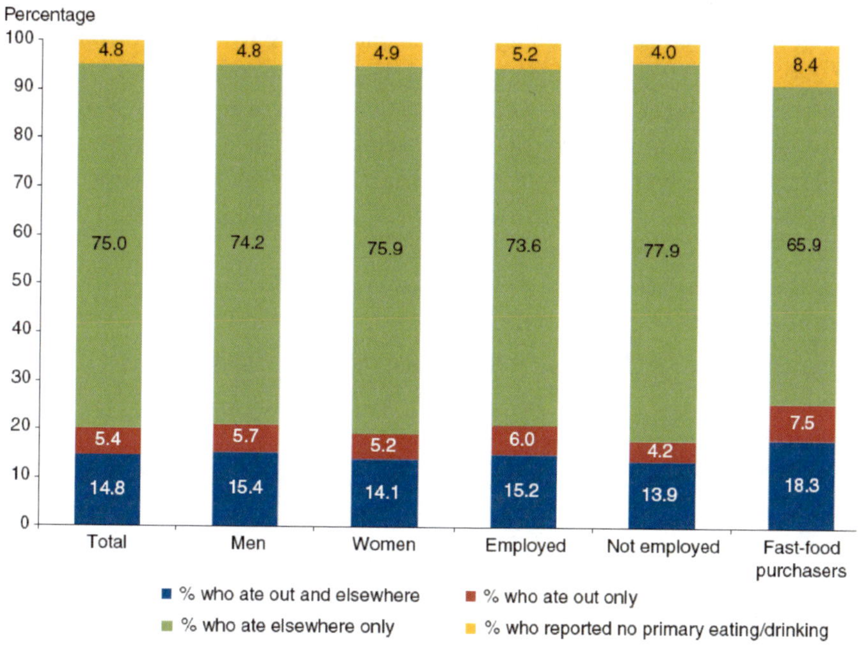

Source: USDA, Economic Research Service estimates calculated from American Time Use Survey data.

Figure 3. Distribution of eating behaviors, 2003-11, age 18 and olderSource:

However, 20.5 percent of those employed ate at a sit-down restaurant on the average day in 2003-11, a higher rate than those not employed (17.4 percent), although the average amount of time spent at the restaurant was about the same for the two groups, about 71 minutes. Similarly, 15.2 percent of those employed also purchased fast food, compared with only 8.8 percent of those not employed.

Of particular interest is time use among those who purchased fast food. Compared with averages for the total population, fast-food purchasers spent less time in primary eating/drinking, sleeping,[6] meal preparation and cleanup and other household activities, and watching television, and more time in caring for household and nonhousehold members and in paid work and accompanying travel. Fast-food purchasers were considerably more likely than the total population to report no primary eating/ drinking (8.4 percent versus 4.8 percent) and more likely to report that all their eating/drinking was at an eating-out establishment (7.5 percent versus 5.4 percent) (Figure 3).

Because fast-food purchasers are more likely to report no primary eating/drinking, there was the possibility that they engage in more secondary eating, that is, eating while doing another "main" activity. Based on data from the 2006-08 ATUS Eating & Health Module, fast-food purchasers spent about the same amount of time in secondary eating on an average day as the total population (23.1 minutes versus 23.9 minutes) but more time in secondary drinking (76.9 minutes versus 65.4 minutes). In addition, fast-food purchasers were more likely to engage in secondary eating or drinking while at work or driving a vehicle than non-fast-food purchasers.

CHANGES BEFORE AND AFTER THE BUSINESS CYCLE PEAK

The National Bureau of Economic Research dates the last U.S. business cycle peak as December 2007, the end of an expansion, and the beginning of a recession that would last until the business cycle trough June 2009, ending the Great Recession. Although a new expansion started at the trough, economic recovery was slow post-recession, and, in particular, the labor market was slow to recover. It was not until May 2014 that the economy recovered the 8.7 million jobs lost during the recession, fully 5 years after the trough. Although time-use patterns change little if any year to year, the economic impact of a recession, especially one with the depth of the 2007-09 recession, would be expected to cause changes in Americans' activities due to higher unemployment, lower household income, lower consumer confidence, and other factors, such as a decreased rate of household formation.[7]

In this study, we analyzed the time-use patterns of Americans during January 2003-November 2007 (the ATUS data available for the 2001-07 expansion) and during December 2007-December 2011 (post-Great Recession peak)[8] (Table 1). For the total population, time-use patterns reveal small but systematic changes in Americans' time-use patterns from one period to the next—less time, on average, spent in paid work and in travel; more time spent in meal preparation; less time spent in making purchases as households' discretionary income decreased or households' uncertainty about future income caused them to cut back on spending; and more time watching television. However, average time spent in primary eating/drinking stayed essentially the same in both periods, but the amount of time spent eating out decreased and the amount of time spent eating elsewhere (e.g., at home, at work) increased.

The share of the population who reported no primary eating/drinking on an average day dropped from 5.1 percent pre-peak to 4.5 percent post-peak (Table 2). Although the difference in these estimates is statistically significant, this drop is likely due to a statistical artifact—the ATUS had a large number of respondents (9 percent) who reported no primary eating/drinking in the first year of the survey (2003). As a result, changes were made in the survey instrument in 2004. The share of the population with no primary eating/drinking has been consistently lower in the years that followed.

Among the differences in pre- and post-peak changes between men and women, the most notable is the increase in men's meal preparation time from 17.0 to 19.2 minutes. This finding is consistent with Berik and Kongar (2013), who found that gender difference in housework hours narrowed during the recession from a small increase in fathers' unpaid work and a decrease in mothers' unpaid work.

Time-use patterns of fast-food purchasers were fairly stable between the two periods and exhibited less change than those of the total population. Particularly striking is that the share of fast-food purchasers who ate at a sit-down or fast-food restaurant stayed about the same, while the share of the total population who ate out declined.

The rate of eating out at sit-down restaurants declined from 20.4 percent of the population on an average day pre-peak to 18.4 percent post-peak (Table 2). With the rate of fast-food purchase staying essentially the same, 13.2 to 12.8 percent (not a statistically significant difference), Americans maintained their pattern of purchasing fast food, despite or because of the recession.

The share of the population age 18 and older purchasing fast food on an average day appears to have trended upward between 2003 and 2005 but then leveled off and declined slightly in 2011 (Figure 4). The rate at which these individuals purchased food from sit-down restaurants, however, appears to be in secular decline since before the recession began, at the start of the financial crisis in February 2007 (Federal Reserve Bank of St. Louis, 2014). So, despite the decline in 2011, it appears that the fast-food rate weathered the recession better than the sit-down rate.

Table 1. Time spent in various activities on an average day, 2003-11, age 18 and older, by time period, in minutes

	Total				Men				Women			
	Pre-BCP		Post-BCP		Pre-BCP		Post-BCP		Pre-BCP		Post-BCP	
Number of observations	67,746		50,059		29,017		21,734		38,729		28,325	
Eating and drinking	67.4	[±.37]	67.5	[±.54]	69.5	[±.60]	69.7	[±.74]	65.6	[±.49]	65.3	[±.73]
Eating/drinking out	14.7	[±.30]	13.4	[±.32]	15.0	[±.48]	13.9	[±.47]	14.4	[±.40]	12.9	[±.46]
Sit-down restaurant	14.4	[±.30]	13.0	[±.31]	14.8	[±.47]	13.5	[±.46]	14.1	[±.39]	12.5	[±.45]
Fast food/carryout	0.3	[±.03]	0.4	[±.04]	0.3	[±.04]	0.4	[±.07]	0.3	[±.05]	0.4	[±.07]
Eating/drinking elsewhere	52.7	[±.37]	54.1	[±.47]	54.4	[±.57]	55.8	[±.66]	51.2	[±.44]	52.4	[±.64]
Personal care:												
Sleep	511.1	[±1.04]	517.2	[±1.22]	505.9	[±1.70]	512.2	[±1.74]	515.9	[±1.44]	521.8	[±1.62]
Other personal care	45.8	[±.50]	46.0	[±.59]	38.2	[±.75]	38.0	[±.86]	52.9	[±.68]	53.5	[±.90]
HH activities:												
Meal prep and cleanup	32.8	[±.39]	34.2	[±.47]	17.0	[±.43]	19.2	[±.55]	47.5	[±.60]	48.3	[±.74]
Other HH activities	80.0	[±.88]	75.4	[±1.08]	66.4	[±1.44]	63.9	[±1.50]	92.6	[±1.21]	86.1	[±1.48]
Caring activities:												
Caring for HH members	29.2	[±.51]	27.8	[±.61]	18.0	[±.52]	18.2	[±.78]	39.6	[±.78]	36.8	[±.83]
Caring for non-HH members	10.2	[±.40]	9.2	[±.50]	8.7	[±.59]	8.0	[±.63]	11.6	[±.57]	10.3	[±.63]
Work-related activities	216.8	[±1.71]	208.2	[±2.28]	262.1	[±2.90]	248.1	[±3.44]	174.8	[±1.94]	170.8	[±2.93]
Educational activities	13.9	[±.70]	14.3	[±.97]	12.8	[±1.05]	13.1	[±1.33]	14.9	[±.86]	15.4	[±1.26]
Purchases:												
Grocery purchases	6.4	[±.15]	6.5	[±.19]	4.4	[±.19]	4.8	[±.23]	8.3	[±.21]	8.1	[±.28]
Other purchases	25.2	[±.45]	23.1	[±.45]	20.0	[±.64]	18.6	[±.65]	30.0	[±.67]	27.3	[±.72]
Fast-food/carryout purchases	1.6	[±.04]	1.5	[±.04]	1.6	[±.06]	1.6	[±.07]	1.5	[±.06]	1.5	[±.06]
Volunteer activities	16.1	[±.42]	17.7	[±.56]	13.9	[±.62]	15.5	[±.75]	18.0	[±.56]	19.9	[±.86]

	Total				Men				Women			
	Pre-BCP		Post-BCP		Pre-BCP		Post-BCP		Pre-BCP		Post-BCP	
Leisure activities:												
Watching television	156.7	[±1.25]	167.9	[±1.52]	170.2	[±2.06]	183.3	[±2.33]	144.2	[±1.36]	153.6	[±2.04]
Other leisure	118.7	[±1.13]	114.6	[±1.36]	118.4	[±1.97]	112.1	[±2.03]	119.0	[±1.43]	117.0	[±1.76]
Sports and excercise	17.9	[±.50]	17.8	[±.54]	23.2	[±.82]	23.4	[±.96]	12.9	[±.53]	12.7	[±.49]
Communication	6.3	[±.21]	6.2	[±.22]	3.4	[±.18]	3.7	[±.26]	9.0	[±.32]	8.5	[±.34]
Travel	76.2	[±.70]	72.3	[±.70]	79.2	[±1.16]	75.0	[±1.09]	73.4	[±.86]	69.9	[±.94]
Other activities NEC	9.2	[±.33]	14.0	[±.48]	8.7	[±.53]	13.3	[±.75]	9.6	[±.42]	14.7	[±.62]
Number of observations	8,739		6,383		44,685		31,766		23,061		18,293	
Eating and drinking	56.9	[±1.17]	57.6	[±1.22]	65.8	[±.43]	66.0	[±.68]	70.9	[±.72]	70.1	[±.86]
Eating/drinking out	16.4	[±.88]	16.3	[±.93]	15.2	[±.38]	14.3	[±.41]	13.7	[±.49]	11.7	[±.44]
Sit-down restaurant	14.1	[±.85]	13.2	[±.89]	14.9	[±.38]	13.9	[±.41]	13.4	[±.48]	11.3	[±.44]
Fast food/carryout	2.2	[±.25]	3.1	[±.33]	0.3	[±.04]	0.4		0.4	[±.07]	0.4	[±.08]
Eating/drinking elsewhere	40.5	[±.92]	41.3	[±1.04]	50.6	[±.43]	51.7	[±.56]	57.1	[±.70]	58.4	[±.77]
Personal care:												
Sleep	488.7	[±2.97]	493.7	[±3.24]	494.8	[±1.36]	499.1	[±1.55]	544.6	[±1.85]	550.4	[±2.24]
Other personal care	45.5	[±.83]	47.3	[±1.21]	45.4	[±.48]	45.7	[±.64]	46.8	[±1.08]	46.5	[±1.28]
HH activities:												
Meal prep and cleanup	19.7	[±.84]	20.4	[±1.01]	25.2	[±.40]	27.0	[±.45]	48.5	[±.90]	47.5	[±1.06]
Other HH activities	62.9	[±2.25]	57.7	[±2.49]	65.5	[±.95]	62.0	[±1.06]	109.9	[±1.94]	99.9	[±2.25]
Caring activities:												
Caring for HH members	30.4	[±1.31]	30.2	[±1.78]	27.0		26.1	[±.68]	33.8	[±1.20]	31.0	[±1.12]
Caring for non-HH members	11.5	[±1.17]	11.0	[±1.10]	8.3	[±.46]	7.4	[±.46]	14.2	[±.75]	12.6	[±1.04]
Work-related activities	247.5	[±5.89]	233.8	[±7.11]	319.2	[±2.31]	315.6	[±2.96]	6.8	[±.71]	10.6	[±.94]
Educational activities	19.0	[±2.46]	18.3	[±2.81]	11.5	[±.71]	11.7	[±1.09]	18.8	[±1.59]	19.1	[±1.73]
Purchases:												

Table 1. (Continued)

	Total				Men				Women			
	Pre-BCP		Post-BCP		Pre-BCP		Post-BCP		Pre-BCP		Post-BCP	
Grocery purchases	5.3	[±.35]	5.7	[±.43]	5.5	[±.17]	5.5	[±.21]	8.3	[±.31]	8.3	[±.38]
Other purchases	43.8	[±1.43]	41.7	[±1.47]	23.3	[±.46]	21.3	[±.51]	29.1	[±.84]	26.4	[±.85]
Fast food/carryout purchases	11.6	[±.18]	11.7	[±.22]	1.8	[±.06]	1.8		1.1		1.1	[±.06]
Volunteer activities	17.8	[±1.65]	18.3	[±1.74]	13.4	[±.47]	14.6	[±.57]	21.5	[±.87]	23.5	[±1.04]
Leisure activities:												
Watching television	128.7	[±2.96]	135.5	[±3.94]	125.8	[±1.18]	132.1	[±1.60]	220.2	[±2.85]	233.9	[±2.98]
Other leisure	113.3	[±3.17]	116.8	[±3.84]	96.1	[±1.19]	91.9	[±1.45]	165.1	[±2.45]	156.4	[±2.66]
Sports and excercise	22.2	[±1.49]	20.9	[±1.59]	17.7	[±.62]	17.8	[±.71]	18.2	[±.80]	18.0	[±.88]
Communication	7.4	[±.61]	7.5	[±.74]	5.0	[±.21]	4.7	[±.23]	9.0	[±.39]	9.0	[±.48]
Travel	110.4	[±2.29]	111.1	[±2.27]	83.4	[±.78]	80.5	[±.83]	61.4	[±1.29]	57.3	[±1.17]
Other activities NEC	9.0	[±1.21]	12.8	[±1.23]	7.3	[±.39]	11.0		13.1	[±.64]	19.5	[±1.06]

Notes: NEC = not elsewhere classified. HH = household. BCP = business cycle peak. 90-percent confidence interval in brackets. Eating out is defined as primary eating/drinking at the ATUS locations restaurant or bar, grocery store, other store/mall, and other place. Eating elsewhere is any other place, including at home or at the workplace. The pre-BCP time period is January 2003 to November 2007, and the post-BCP time period is December 2007 to December 2011. *Fast-food purchasers are individuals with at least one fast-food purchase.

Source: USDA, Economic Research Service estimates using American Time Use Survey (ATUS) data.

Table 7.2 Wage equations in the monopsonistic groups

Branch	Group	α	β_0	β_1
3	4	−0.634459	1.096537*	0.014819****
		(2.3970)	(0.3242)	(0.0100)
5	1	−5.750761	1.757105*	0.050564*
		(4.0232)	(0.5606)	(0.0138)
7	2	1.681217	0.681891****	0.107442*
		(3.4329)	(0.4295)	(0.0370)
8	2	4.505140*	0.366078*	0.018554****
		(0.4361)	(0.0557)	(0.0127)
13	2	1.330855	0.770887*	0.035942**
		(1.1574)	(0.1550)	(0.0154)
13	5	−1.650853	1.166414*	0.036877***
		(1.4227)	(0.1895)	(0.0198)
14	1	−0.755032	1.040499****	0.049948****
		(4.7759)	(0.6615)	(0.0330)
14	6	2.990584	0.513126****	0.095826*
		(2.3125)	(0.3233)	(0.0248)
16	6	−2.357617	1.242574**	0.070620*
		(4.2420)	(0.5821)	(0.0190)
18	5	1.407162***	0.752771*	0.0499****
		(0.7827)	(0.1059)	(0.0330)

Notes: * Significant at a 1% level; ** significant at a 5% level; *** significant at a 10% level; **** significant at a 15% level; standard errors in brackets.

productivity–wage exploitation rates (groups 5 and 6). That is to say that they should not be supposed to be monopsonistic, given our first test. We can further observe that these firms always pay workers less than the average sector wage, that is that they probably employ lower skilled workers. As we will see further, it is likely that the accounting data we use underestimate actual workers value added, in these sectors. So estimated mark-ups in these groups could be underestimated.

A third remark is to remember that estimating positive β_1 should also reflect efficiency wages rather than monopsony. We think our results better support the second assumption for two reasons:

- firms belong, in nine cases out of ten, to groups paying wages that are lower than average wages in the branch activity. It does not seem that consistent with the efficiency wages assumption;
- if we observe employment structure in these firms, we note that 60 per cent of firms occupy less than 100 workers. As efficiency wages are generally estimated to be more present in bigger firms, our facts do not support this assumption.

Explaining monopsonistic behaviour by activity branch

It is not necessarily easy to give a clear answer for each of the eight branches where we suggest monopsonistic presence in some groups of firms belonging to these branches. We will comment on three of them.

Considering the international leaderships in the chemical branch (Le Dortz and Perrochon, 2001), we can probably assume that some firms have market power. If they train their labour force in specific occupations, they can limit labour mobility and possess thereby some monopsonistic power.

The other hotels and restaurants branch is often considered to propose secondary jobs to seasonal and lower skilled workers, who can probably be more subject to monopsonistic behaviour.

Finally, the building industry branch could partly occupy 'black' jobs. This capacity could make easier to develop a peculiar management of declared human resources. More precisely, the 'black' labour force could be used as a downward wage-pressure against the declared labour force.

Considering hotels and restaurants or building branches, the Belgian Economic Central Council (2001, 2002) further points the fact that there seems to be a shortage in labour supply availability. The fact that some firms of these branches could exert monopsonistic behaviour could also explain this basic observation.

Further developments on monopsonistic behaviour. A segmented approach

Monopsonistic behaviour by skills

Though we are not excluding the assumption of monopsonistic behaviour among firms that employ higher skilled workers, we estimate that only one group of firms, precisely in the branch 'Food, beverage and tobacco', employs workers that receive higher than average wages. That is to say that monopsonistic behaviour seems merely to apply to lower skilled workers, that is to say receiving lower than average wages.

We want to shed some additional light on this relation. We are therefore interested in getting data on the labour force by another better proxy for skills, missing in our main dataset. Therefore, we use another dataset, referred as the Belgian social outcome, where we can find information about skills of workers hired during a given period of time. It is in fact compulsory for firms to complete this social outcome since 1996. We are therefore able to analyse these data during the period 1996–99. Note that inflows in monopsonistic firms represent 6.62 per cent of the total.

We can calculate, for each branch in our sample, the average proportion of lower and higher skilled workers inflows, lower skills when workers do not possess higher than six years equivalent secondary school level, higher skills in other cases. For the branches where some groups are supposed to be monopsonists, we calculated proportions by skills in each of these groups.

For simplicity, we would not reproduce data related to the relative lower/higher skilled proportions for the different groups or branches. They are available on request. We will just mention that, if we calculate the mean proportion of low skilled on the overall firms, we obtain a level of 77.38 per cent. Coming to monopsonistic firms, they employ on average relatively more lower skilled workers, except for firms which belong to two out of ten groups.

Considering lower skilled proportions, we have then tested the independence of means between monopsonistic and non-monopsonistic firms using a *t*-test. The sample to which the test is performed is detailed in Table 7.3. Monopsonistic firms are grouped as number 1, non-monopsonistic as number 0. Table 7.4 presents the relative proportions for lower skilled workers.

Table 7.5 presents the results of the tests. Note that, to perform the appropriate test of independence of means, we first have to apply the Levene's test for equality of variances, which is significant in our case. We therefore have to consider the test for equality of means of proportions under this first assumption. Row 2 shows that our test significantly rejects the assumption of equality of means, between the two groups of firms. Therefore, our dataset allows to conclude that the observed higher proportion of lower skilled workers in monopsonistic firms (78.6 per cent versus 73.9 per cent) is statistically significant.

This result is important, as it suggests that if monopsonistic behaviour appears, it mostly applies towards lower skilled individuals, and even though this assumption has not been encountered in all but in eight out of ten monopsonistic groups.

Table 7.3 Lower skilled proportions in the inflows among monopsonistic and other firms: statistical data

	Monopsony (1) or not (0)	Number of firms	Mean (%)	Std. dev. (%)	Std. error mean (%)
Lower skilled	1	275	78.5739	21.0619	1.2701
	0	6.070	73.8633	30.0577	0.3858

Table 7.4 Testing for equal skill levels proportions in inflows between monopsonistic and other firms

		Levene's test for equality of variances		*t*-test for equality of means			
		F	Sig.	*t*	df	Sig. (2-tailed)	Mean difference (%)
Lower skilled proportions	Equal variances assumed	54.560	0.000	2.570	6.343	0.010	4.7106
	Equal variances not assumed			3.549	326.771	0.000	4.7106

Table 7.5 Age proportions among monopsonistic and other branches: statistical data

	Monopsony (1) or not (0)	Number of branches	Mean (%)	Std. dev. (%)	Std. error mean (%)
<25 years old	1	8	13.93	7.917	2.799
	0	16	10.09	5.172	1.293
>29 years old	1	8	70.27	10.22	3.613
	0	16	75.32	7.938	1.984

Monopsonistic behaviour by age

Besides skills level, another important point we want to investigate is whether monopsonistic behaviour is differentiated between labour suppliers segmented by age. As a matter of fact, the unemployment level of individuals is roughly twice as much for 25-year-old individuals as it is for the elders.

To segment workers by age, we can only use another dataset of employment built by the Social Security Office. It considers, for each sector, the employed labour force for 13 categories of age. We have grouped these data in three age categories for the 24 selected activity branches. These data unfortunately do not permit to divide branches by groups. So we cannot calculate relative proportions of young individuals in the monopsonistic groups, but only in aggregate branches that sometimes include groups of monopsonistic firms.

Coming back to the proportions of less than 25-year-old individuals working in the branches with groups of monopsonistic firms, we notice that these proportions (available on request) are quite stable in time, and that they are much more important that in the other non-monopsonistic branches. On average, young individuals represent, for example, 16.9 per cent in monopsonistic branches in 1997, only 10.4 per cent in the others. That is to say that we could probably assume that monopsony is more present among inflows of young workers, that it could better represent a first job phenomenon rather than a practice towards older more stabilised labour force.

We still performed the *t*-test of independence of means by age between monopsonistic and non-monopsonistic branches. Table 7.5 presents statistical data for less than 25 years and more than 29 years proportions, while Table 7.6 contains the relevant Levene's and *t*-tests for different means of proportions between branches with some or no monopsonistic groups of firms.

Table 7.6 Testing for age proportions between monopsonistic and other branches

		Levene's test for equality of variances		***t*-test for equality of means**			
		F	**Sig.**	*t*	df	**Sig. (2-tailed)**	**Mean difference**
<25-year-old proportions	Equal variances assumed	0.720	**0.405**	1.437	22	**0.165**	0.0385
	Equal variances not assumed			1.247	10.092	0.241	0.0385
>29-year-old proportions	Equal variances assumed	0.131	**0.721**	−1.336	22	**0.195**	−0.0505
	Equal variances not assumed			−1.225	11.376	0.245	−0.0505

We can observe from Table 7.5 that proportions of less than 25-year-old individuals are higher in monopsonistic branches, while older than 29-year-old individuals are more represented in the non-monopsonistic ones. These differences are quite close to be, but are not statistically significant when we look at the *t*-test in Table 7.6. Note that this lack of significance is likely to be related to the small number of observations we unfortunately had to consider.

To conclude and even if the *t*-test does not necessarily allow to statistically validate this proposition, the comparison between monopsonistic and non-monopsonistic branches suggests that monopsonistic firms employ an higher proportion of young workers than the others.

5 Conclusion

In terms of active labour market policies and especially when people investigates how deregulation can be an efficient way to get rid of unemployment, it is crucial to estimate whether this labour shortage has to be related to some kind of imperfect competition on the labour market.

Using a labour demand type of framework, we precisely wanted to estimate whether imperfect competition has to be related to monopsonistic behaviour of firms, and to what extent. We remarked that Belgian empirical facts do not necessarily support the assumption of monopsony as a generalised practice. But some institutional facts could still allow firms to have some power, for example, when they can classify a worker under his actual productivity, when they can pay wages fixed at a sectoral level but that are under the productivity of their labour force or when they can benefit from government regulated wages.

We developed a model coming to the end that maximising profit firms should benefit from a positive exploitation rate, that is to say a positive productivity–wage gap, when they possess monopsonistic power. So our first goal was to estimate exploitation rates. But we noticed that positive exploitation rates can also be present in other situations than monopsony, like when firms possess a market power on the product market. So we also control for this other possibility. Moreover, given that positive exploitation rates are not a sufficient condition to conclude, we performed another test, though still not decisive, which basically assumes that wages should be positively related to employment levels in case of monopsony. Finally, besides testing for monopsonistic power existence, we also wanted to differentiate this behaviour by skills and age of the labour force.

To perform the tests from a labour demand point of view, we considered a first balanced panel of 6585 firms. We estimated the exploitation rates assuming a Cobb–Douglass technology and the wage–employment relationship using a Generalised Least Squares estimation technique with a correction for random individual fixed effects.

Though our tests are not conclusive, we think that our results strengthen the assumption of partial monopsonistic behaviour, that is to say among some firms. Our first test classified 20.2 per cent of firms in groups where monopsonistic behaviour could alone, that is to say after controlling for product market power, explain positive exploitation rates. Our second test estimates that monopsonistic behaviour could apply to firms occupying 8.32 per cent of the labour force. We mentioned that monopsony could be more important than that, if we did not had to estimate our relations by considering groups of firms classified in a rather usual 'arbitrary' sectoral way. This remark appeals for further research on how monopsonistic firms can be better identified. It is also worth to mention that our results related to the second test better support monopsony, rather than efficiency wages, as an explanation of the positive relation between wages and employment.

In terms of monopsony related to segmented labour supply, we first significantly concluded that monopsonistic behaviour does seem to be proportionally linked to lower skilled workers to a bigger extent. We were not able to significantly confirm a positive relation between monopsonistic behaviour and the age of individuals, though we observe mean proportions of young individuals that are more important in branches that contain some monopsonistic groups of firms.

These results still rest on rather strong assumptions and ask for better datasets and controls. But they are not necessarily refuted by institutional facts. They support the idea that deregulating the labour market could not necessarily be positive for employment, at least in some firms, remembering on the other hand that deregulation probably worsens at the same time the well-being of the workers.

References

Allaart, P. (2002) 'Wage Differentials Between and Within Establishments: An Eclectic Approach', *Proceedings of the 79th International Applied Econometrics Association*, Brussels, Belgium.

Belgian Economic Central Council (2001) 'Construction 2000–2001: de l'optimisme à la prudence', *Lettre socio-économique*, pp. 3–10.

Belgian Economic Central Council (2002) 'L'emploi dans le secteur Horeca: aspects quantitatifs et qualitatifs', *Rapport de la Commission Horeca*, p. 11.

Blanchflower, D. and Freeman, R. (1994) 'Did the Thatcher Reforms Change British Labour Performance?', in Barrell, R. (ed.), *The UK Labour Market: Comparative Aspects and Institutional Developments*, Cambridge, UK: Cambridge University Press, pp. 51–72.

Blundell, R. (1993) 'Offre de travail et fiscalité: une revue de la littérature', *Economie et Prévision*, 108(2), pp. 1–18.

Blundell, R. and McCurdy, T. (1999) 'Labor Supply: A Review of Alternative Approaches', in Ashenfelter, O. and Card, D. (eds) *Handbook of Labor Economics*, Elsevier Science Publisher, 3A, chapter 27, pp. 1559–695.

Boadway, R. and Cuff, K. (2001) 'A Minimum Wage can be Welfare-improving and Employment-enhancing', *European Economic Review*, 45(3), pp. 553–76.

Boal, W. (1995) 'Testing for Employer Monopsony in Turn-of-the-Century Coal Mining', *Rand Journal of Economy*, 26(3), pp. 519–36.

Boal, W. and Ransom, M. (1997) 'Monopsony in the Labor Market', *The Journal of Economic Literature*, 35(1), pp. 86–112.

Brown, R. (1993) 'An Estimate of the Rent Generated by a Premium College Football Player', *Economic Inquiry*, 31(4), pp. 671–84.

Burdett, K. and Mortensen, D. (1998) 'Wage Differentials, Employer Size, and Unemployment', *International Economic Review*, 39(2), pp. 257–73.

Cahuc, P. and Zylberberg, A. (2001) *Le marché du travail*, De Boeck Université, p. 714.

Dolado, J., Kramarz, F., Machin, S., Manning, A., Margolis, D. and Teulings, C. (1996) 'The Economic Impact of Minimum Wages in Europe', *Economic Policy*, 23, pp. 317–57.

Gregg, P. and Manning, A. (1997) 'Labour Market Regulation and Unemployment', in Snower, D. and de la Dehesa, G. (eds) *Unemployment Policy: Government Options for the Labour Market*, Cambridge, UK: Cambridge University Press, pp. 395–429.

Le Dortz, L. and Perrochon, D. (2001) 'Stratégies des fusions-acquisitions 2000 dans la chimie et la pharmacie: un secteur qui se réinvente', Centre Français du Commerce Extérieur, Paris, p. 75.

Lindbeck, A. and Snower, D.J. (1989) 'The Insider–Outsider Theory of Employment and Unemployment', Cambridge, MA: MIT Press, p. 285.

Luizer, J. and Thornton, R. (1986) 'Concentration in the Local Labor Market for Public School Teachers', *Industrial and Labour Relations Review*, 39(4), pp. 573–84.

Manning, A. (1995) 'How do we Know that Real Wages are too High?', *Quarterly Journal of Economics*, 110(4), pp. 1111–25.

Manning, A. (2001) 'A Generalised Model of Monopsony', *Centre for Economic Performance Discussion Papers*, 499, p. 21.

Masters, A. (1999) 'Wage Posting in Two-sided Search and the Minimum Wage', *International Economic Review*, 40(4), pp. 809–26.

Ransom, M. (1993) 'Seniority and Monopsony in the Labor Market', *American Economic Review*, 83(1), pp. 221–33.

Rebitzer, J. and Taylor, L. (1995) 'The Consequences of Minimum Wage Laws, Some New Theoretical Ideas', *Journal of Public Economics*, 56(2), pp. 245–55.

Robinson, J. (1969) *The Economics of Imperfect Competition*, 2nd edition, London: Macmillan, p. 352.

Scully, G.W. (1974) 'Pay and Performance in Major League BaseBall', *American Economic Review*, 64(6), pp. 915–30.

Table 2. Participation rates and distribution of eating behaviors, 2003-11, age 18 and older, by time period

	Total				Men				Women			
	Pre-BCP		Post-BCP		Pre-BCP		Post-BCP		Pre-BCP		Post-BCP	
Participation rates (percent) and time spent by participants (minutes):												
% who ate out, sit-down	20.4	[±.34]	18.4	[±.37]	21.2	[±.54]	19.5	[±.57]	19.6	[±.46]	17.4	[±.53]
Ave. time spent eating at sit down	70.7	[±.76]	70.5	[±.92]	69.6	[±1.21]	69.0	[±1.33]	71.9	[±.97]	72.0	[±1.29]
% who purchased fast food/carryout	13.2	[±.30]	12.8	[±.33]	13.8	[±.47]	13.0	[±.51]	12.5	[±.36]	12.6	[±.43]
Ave. time spent in purchasing FF	11.8	[±.18]	11.9	[±.22]	11.7	[±.24]	12.0	[±.33]	11.9	[±.24]	11.8	[±.28]
% who ate out, FF restaurant	0.8	[±.08]	1.0	[±.10]	0.7	[±.10]	1.0	[±.16]	0.8	[±.10]	1.0	[±.13]
Ave. time spent eating at FF	41.2	[±2.04]	42.7	[±2.40]	38.8	[±2.81]	41.4	[±3.16]	43.1	[±2.97]	43.8	[±3.63]
Distribution of eating behaviors:												
% who ate out and elsewhere	15.3	[±.31]	14.1	[±.34]	15.9	[±.48]	14.9	[±.52]	14.8	[±.39]	13.3	[±.50]
% who ate out only	5.7	[±.19]	5.1	[±.19]	5.9	[±.32]	5.3	[±.30]	5.4	[±.25]	4.9	[±.28]
% who ate elsewhere only	74.0	[±.38]	76.3	[±.41]	73.2	[±.57]	75.3	[±.62]	74.7	[±.50]	77.2	[±.60]

Table 2. (Continued)

	Total				Men				Women			
	Pre-BCP		Post-BCP		Pre-BCP		Post-BCP		Pre-BCP		Post-BCP	
% who reported no primary E/D	5.1	[±.18]	4.5	[±.22]	5.1	[±.25]	4.4	[±.30]	5.1	[±.25]	4.7	[±.31]
	Fast-food purchasers				Employed				Not employed			
	Pre-BCP		Post-BCP		Pre-BCP		Post-BCP		Pre-BCP		Post-BCP	
Participation rates (percent) and time spent by participants (minutes):												
% who ate out, sit-down	21.0	[±.96]	20.2	[±1.16]	21.3	[±.42]	19.6	[±.47]	18.6	[±.54]	16.2	[±.53]
Ave. time spent eating at sit-down	67.4	[±2.21]	65.0	[±2.25]	70.2	[±.95]	70.9	[±1.16]	72.1	[±1.39]	69.6	[±1.36]
% who purchased fast food/carryout	98.0*	[±.32]	97.7*	[±.34]	15.2	[±.39]	15.1	[±.46]	8.9	[±.45]	8.5	[±.41]
Ave. time spent in purchasing FF	11.8	[±.18]	11.9	[±.22]	11.5	[±.21]	11.7	[±.25]	12.8	[±.39]	12.6	[±.45]
% who ate out, FF restaurant	5.4	[±.56]	7.3	[±.74]	0.7	[±.09]	1.0	[±.13]	0.8	[±.15]	0.9	[±.13]
Ave. time spent eating at FF	41.5	[±2.11]	42.9	[±2.44]	39.7	[±2.35]	40.4	[±2.17]	44.0	[±3.89]	47.7	[±5.83]

	Fast-food purchasers				Employed				Not employed			
	Pre-BCP		Post-BCP		Pre-BCP		Post-BCP		Pre-BCP		Post-BCP	
Distribution of eating behaviors:												
% who ate out and elsewhere	17.7	[±.96]	19.0	[±1.16]	15.6	[±.39]	14.6	[±.44]	14.7	[±.48]	13.2	[±.51]
% who ate out only	7.6	[±.66]	7.3	[±.67]	6.2	[±.26]	5.8	[±.25]	4.6	[±.31]	3.7	[±.30]
% who ate elsewhere only	66.1	[±1.20]	65.6	[±1.27]	72.8	[±.47]	74.6	[±.48]	76.4	[±.62]	79.4	[±.65]
% who reported no primary E/D	8.6	[±.70]	8.1	[±.83]	5.4	[±.21]	5.0	[±.29]	4.3	[±.31]	3.7	[±.29]

Notes: FF = fast food. E/D = eating/drinking. BCP = business cycle peak. Confidence interval in brackets. Eating out is defined as primary eating/drinking at the ATUS locations restaurant or bar, grocery store, other store/mall, and other place. Eating elsewhere is any other place, such as at home or at the workplace. The pre-recession period is January 2003 to November 2007, and the mid/post-recession period is December 2007 to December 2011. *Percent who purchased fast food/carryout is not 100 percent because some individuals do not report purchase time, only eating/drinking time. Here, the category "Only those who purchased fast food" includes those with zero purchase time but some fast-food eating/drinking time.

Source: USDA, Economic Research Service estimates using American Time Use Survey (ATUS) data.

For individuals who are employed, the moving average fast-food participation rate stayed fairly level since the start of the recession whereas the sit-down rate declined (figs. 5a and 5b). Both rates appear to have declined for those not employed. Not surprisingly, both sit-down and fast-food rates are lower for those not employed than for those employed.

Overall, the summary statistics show fast-food and sit-down purchasing behavior varied by gender and employment status in that men and those employed purchased more fast food and sit-down food than women and those not employed. Also, fast-food purchasers had very different time-use patterns than the total population, with fast-food purchasers spending less time in eating and drinking, meal preparation and other household activities, and watching television but more time in caring for household members and in paid work. Over the business cycle, fast-food purchase behavior in terms of the share of the population purchasing fast food on an average day held fairly steady through and after the recession, while the share eating at sit-down restaurants declined. While there may seem to be certain associations between fast-food purchasing behavior and gender, employment, and time use, many other factors changed over the study period that may confound any associations discussed here.

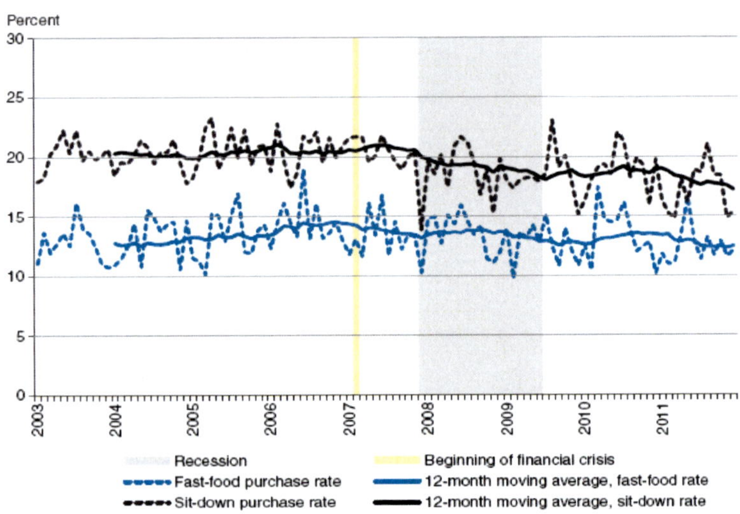

Source: USDA, Economic Research Service estimates calculated from American Time Use Survey data.

Figure 4. Participation rates of fast-food and sit-down purchasers, age 18 and older Percent.

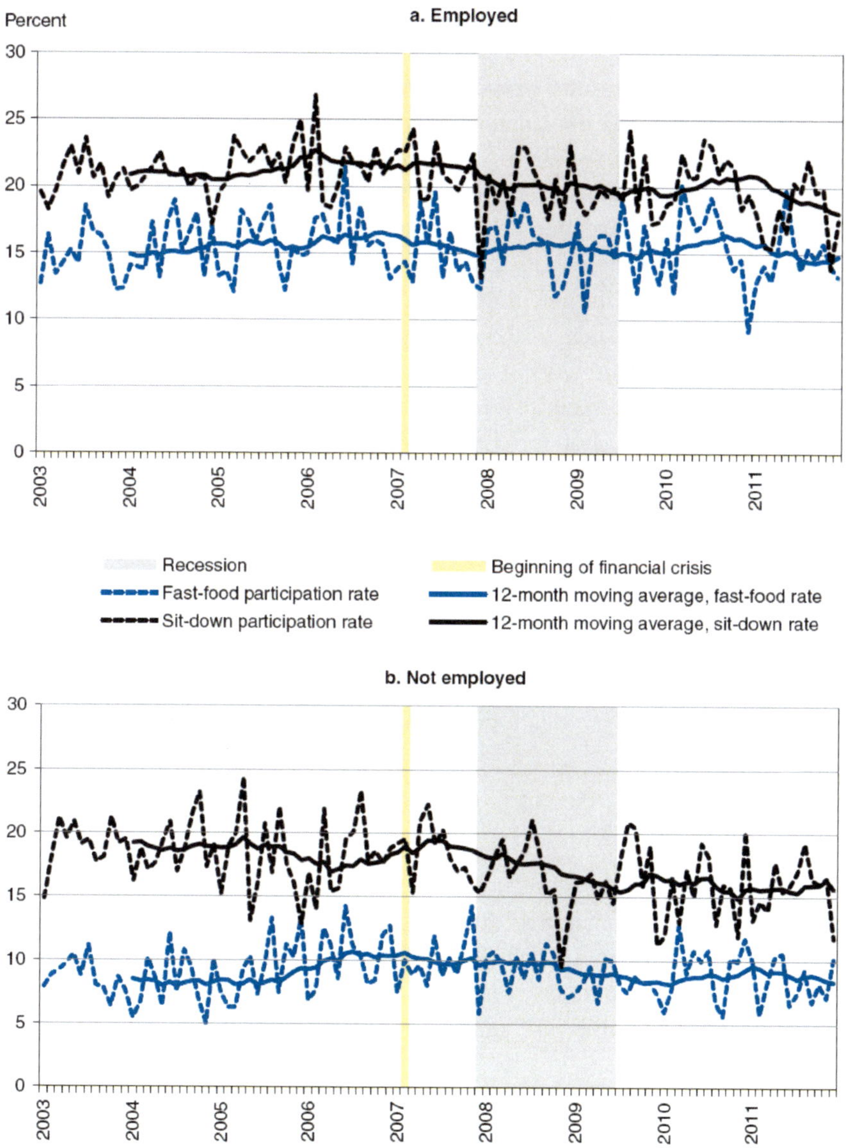

Source: USDA, Economic Research Service estimates calculated from American Time Use Survey data.

Figure 5. Participation rates of fast-food and sit-down purchasers, age 18 and older, by employment status.

MULTIVARIATE ANALYSIS

The descriptive results provide a motivation for multivariate treatment because many of the explanatory factors are correlated, which makes it difficult to determine the direct associations of these factors. For example, fast-food purchase appears to be related to employment and also to time spent in travel. However, those who are employed tend to spend more time in travel on an average day than those not employed, as travel includes their work commute. In addition, fast-food purchasers tend to spend less time than others in certain activities, such as household tasks and watching television, but spend more time in paid work. Lastly, men are more likely than women to eat out and are also more likely to be employed. As a consequence, time patterns are interrelated with labor force status and demographic characteristics, and with fast-food purchasing behavior as well.

We modeled whether individual j purchased fast food, y_j, as a function of a matrix of demographic, employment status, and household composition characteristics of individual j ($\boldsymbol{D}_j$), the value of time as proxied by time spent in market labor, household, and leisure activities ($\boldsymbol{W}_i$), geographic covariates including price for market m ($\boldsymbol{M}_{mt}$), which vary over time, t, and household income (V_j).[9] Note that we modeled whether the individual, not the household, purchased fast food. Specifically, we adopted a probit model such that

$$p_j = \Pr[y_j = 1 \mid \mathbf{D}_j, \mathbf{W}_j, \mathbf{M}_{mt}, V_j] = \Phi(\mathbf{D}_j'\beta_1 + \mathbf{W}_j'\beta_2 + \mathbf{M}_{mt}'\beta_3 + V_j\beta_4) \quad (1)$$

where $\Phi(\cdot)$ is the cumulative distribution function for the standard normal distribution. We used a probit model as the vast majority of fast-food purchasers made one purchase on an average day.[10] The marginal effect of the kth explanatory variable, x_k, on the probability of fast-food purchase is calculated as

$$dp_j / dx_k = \phi(\mathbf{X}'\beta)\beta_k \quad (2)$$

where $\mathbf{X}$ is the matrix of $\mathbf{D}_j$, $\mathbf{W}j$, $\mathbf{M}_{mt}$, and V_j, and ö(·) is the density of the standard normal distribution. We evaluated the marginal effects in (2) at the means of the data[11] and used the Delta method to calculate the standard errors of the marginal effects.

Siotis, G. (2000) 'Market Power, Total Factor Productivity Growth, and Structural Change. An Illustration for Spain, 1983–1996', Banco de España, Servicio de Estudios, Documento de Trabajo, no. 0001, pp. 7–45.

Zimbalist, A. (1992) 'Salaries and Performance: Beyond the Scully Model', in Sommers, M.D. (ed.) *Diamonds are Forever: The Business of Baseball*, Washington DC: The Brookings Institution, pp. 109–33.

Index

We proxied the value of time by including indicators for employment and part-time schedule and the amount of time spent at various "necessary" and "committed" activities. Following Kalenkoski et al. (2011), "necessary" activities are sleeping and grooming, whereas "committed" activities are household activities (includes meal preparation), caring for household members, paid work and work-related activities, and travel associated with these activities. These definitions are in line with the time poverty literature.[12] If individuals have greater necessary and committed activities, they may be more likely to purchase fast food due to time pressures. We included time-use variables such as work time (1-12 hours and more than 12 hours), personal care time (sleep and grooming), household activities, care of household children and adults, and total travel time. Indeed, results show that fast-food purchasers spent less time in personal care activities due to less sleep and spent more time in paid work and travel than the total population. This indicates that time constraints are likely a factor in the fast-food purchase decision. We included the recreational activity watching television, which is by far the dominant recreational activity with the longest average time duration (2.7 hours a day) over the total population and usual subgroups.[13] We also included primary eating and drinking time because in Table 2 we found that fast-food purchasers were more likely to have no primary eating/ drinking time over the day, and we wanted to determine if a relationship exists between primary eating/drinking time and fast-food purchases while controlling for other factors.

A problem with several of our time-use variables that proxy for the opportunity cost of time is that they may be endogenous. Endogeneity can arise if the household decision to prepare meals or go out to eat and the time associated with this decision is correlated with omitted variables that capture household production patterns not observed in equation (1).[14] However, it is very difficult to find appropriate instruments for these time-use patterns (Cawley and Liu, 2012). To address the endogeneity that may arise from unobserved differences in household production patterns, we modeled fast-food purchasing behavior by household type (i.e., single person, single parent, couple no children, couple with children, other households no children, and other household with children).[15]

Endogeneity of the time-use variables can arise from division of labor decisions in household production for the different types of households, as they face different preferences and pressures and have different decisionmaking processes. For example, a single-person household would have different meal and snack behavior than a married couple with children. In particular, the individual in the single-person household would make time-use decisions independent of others, as there are no others in the household. An individual in a married or unmarried couple may have meal and snack patterns without meal preparation if the other household member does those tasks. Hence, we estimate the model for the different household types to control for differences in division of labor. In these models, we include proxies for the division of labor decision, the employment status of the spouse/partner, the spouse/partner's usual weekly work hours, or whether the spouse/partner's usual weekly work hours vary. These proxies are in line with the home production literature.[16] We acknowledge that estimation by household type may not completely eliminate the endogeneity issue, and, therefore, we only discuss results as associations between the time-use variables and fast-food purchase behavior in the analysis that follows.

The demographic characteristics include gender, age group, education level, citizenship status, race, and Hispanic ethnicity. Employment status of the respondent is also included to account for potential changes in employment during the Great Recession and its effect on fast-food purchasing status. In the "All" model with all individuals, we included household type and then estimated models for each household type.

We also included several market-level and time-varying variables. We included indicators for Census region and metro/nonmetropolitan area of residence because previous studies found that nonmetro residence would be expected to have a negative relationship with the probability of fast-food purchase due to less access to fast-food establishments. While such regional indicators proxy for price effects, we also included the price of a limited-service meal.[17] This is the average quarterly price of meals and entrees in a Census division at an establishment that does not have table service (Kumcu and Okrent, 2014). We inflated the price to 2011 dollars using the Census region Consumer Price Index for all items (BLS, 2013a). Indicators for quarter and year were included to account for seasonality in eating-out behavior. Also, an indicator of day of week was included—weekday day (Monday through Friday, and not a holiday) and weekend day or holiday (Saturday, Sunday, or holiday). We also included time-trend variables (1-9) because we used pooled cross-section data. Lastly, we included a monthly unemployment rate variable (BLS, 2013b) as well as an indicator of whether the ATUS respondent's diary day occurred during the recession (December 2007-June 2009) or after to capture the effects of the Great Recession.

For household income, we include a fairly blunt variable to define "high-income" for 2003-11, indicating whether the household had income greater than 200 percent of the poverty threshold for a family of four. A more precise indicator was not used because of the difficulty working with the ATUS income variable.[18]

We present the marginal effects at the mean of the data for the probit model in two sections: (1) the entire ATUS sample for the period 2003-11 (Table 3, coefficient estimates in appendix Table 4); and (2) a subsample of the ATUS for the pre-recession period (i.e., January 2003-November 2007) and a subsample for the recession and post-recession period (i.e., December 2007–December 2011) (Table 4). All estimates are weighted to be nationally representative (see appendix Table 3 for the mean values of the variables used in the models).[19]

Analysis of the Entire Sample Period, 2003-11

Looking at the "All" model with individuals from all household types and controlling for other covariates shows many of the demographic variables to be associated with the probability of fast-food purchase. Specifically, individuals age 18-24 were 3.5 percentage points (marginal probability of 0.035) *more* likely to make a fast-food purchase on an average day than the excluded group of individuals age 25-64, and those age 65 or older were 3.7 percentage points *less* likely to purchase fast food. Individuals with more education were more likely to purchase fast food than lesser educated individuals, and the probablity that noncitizens would purchase fast food, with a marginal probability of -0.059, was lower than that of citizens. Although we found a statistically significant difference in the rate of fast-food purchase between men and women in the descriptive statistics, the gender difference was not statistically different from zero after controlling for other factors.

In terms of employment status, those employed were 2.4 percentage points more likely to purchase fast food than those unemployed, although having a part-time work schedule did not seem to make a difference. However, the analysis finds that the association between time spent in paid work on an average day and probability of fast-food purchase was nonlinear and negative. Compared with the excluded group (individuals with 0 minutes of paid work), those who engaged in paid work or work-related activities (such as job search) for some positive amount of time (up to and including 720 minutes, or 12 hours) reduced the marginal probability of purchasing fast food by 1.8 percentage points.

Table 3. Marginal estimates at the mean based on probit model of fast-food purchase, 2003-11, by household type

	All	Single person	Single parent	Couple, no children	Couple with children	Other HH, no children	Other HH with children
Demographic characteristics:							
Female	0.001	-0.023***	0.022	-0.002	0.011	0.006	0.011**
Age 18-24	0.035***	0.036***	-0.020	0.035**	0.019	0.055***	0.022***
Age 65+	-0.037***	-0.031***		-0.017**		-0.044***	-0.038**
Education, less than high school	-0.019***	-0.022**	0.028	-0.022**	-0.017	-0.007	-0.030***
Education, some college	0.013***	0.010	0.017	0.013**	0.011	0.018*	0.008
Education, college degree	0.015***	0.003	0.034**	0.021***	0.005	0.024**	0.006
Education, advanced degree	0.005	0.005	-0.017	0.001	-0.007	0.002	0.011
Noncitizen	-0.059***	-0.038***	-0.074**	-0.028**	-0.071***	-0.060***	-0.075***
African-American/ Black	-0.002	0.004	-0.011	-0.001	0.002	-0.003	-0.008
Asian	-0.028***	-0.033	-0.021	-0.004	-0.022	-0.061**	-0.027**
Mixed race	0.001	0.010	-0.118**	-0.002	-0.005	0.025	-0.020
Hispanic	-0.011**	-0.013	-0.024	0.007	0.005	-0.019	-0.014**

Geographic characteristics:							
Midwest region	-0.059	-0.059	-0.007	0.005	0.015	-0.024*	0.006
South region	-0.002*	-0.002	-0.001	0.004	0.015	-0.001	0.014**
West region	-0.028	-0.028	-0.018	-0.001	0.012	-0.001	0.016**
Nonmetro residence	0.001**	0.001	0.010	-0.001	0.013	-0.013	-0.010*
Labor force characteristics:							
Employed	0.024***	0.021**	0.043**	0.017**	0.010	0.025**	0.027***
Employed part-time schedule:	-0.005	-0.011	-0.024	-0.010	0.053	-0.014	0.001
Household type:							
Single person HH	0.014***						
Single parent HH	0.025***						
Couple with child(ren) HH	0.008						
Other type of HH, with children	0.018***						
Other type of HH, no children	0.012***						
Household characteristics:							
Number in HH			-0.015		0.013	-0.028	-0.006
Number in HH squared	-0.001*		-0.001		-0.002	0.003	0.001

Table 3. (Continued)

	All	Single person	Single parent	Couple, no children	Couple with children	Other HH, no children	Other HH with children
Child less than age 6 in HH	0.001		-0.003		0.017		0.003
Spouse employed				0.017	-0.027		
Spouse's usual weekly work hrs				-0.001	0.001		
Spouse's weekly work hrs vary				-0.028	0.058*		
HH income> 200% poverty threshold	0.020***	0.007	0.014	0.010	0.055***	0.027***	0.025***
HH income value missing	0.018***	0.012	0.007	-0.005	0.049**	0.055***	0.017**
Time use:							
Work and work related, 1-12 hrs	-0.018***	0.002	-0.040**	-0.009	-0.010	-0.025**	-0.027***
Work and work related, >12 hrs	-0.088***	-0.051***	-0.135***	-0.047**	-0.082**	-0.120***	-0.112***
Primary eating/ drinking, hours	-0.034***	-0.029***	-0.032***	-0.028***	-0.028***	-0.033***	-0.044***
Personal care time, hours	-0.007***	-0.006***	-0.008***	-0.006***	-0.006*	-0.009***	-0.006***
Housework, hours	-0.011***	-0.011***	-0.011***	-0.010***	-0.011***	-0.012***	-0.011***
HH child/adult care, hours	-0.001		-0.001	-0.001	-0.003	0.014**	-0.002
Watching TV, hours	-0.004***	-0.006***	-0.003	-0.003***	-0.004	-0.006***	-0.004***
Travel time, hours	0.027***	0.024***	0.035***	0.023***	0.026***	0.025***	0.034***

	All	Single person	Single parent	Couple, no children	Couple with children	Other HH. no children	Other HH with children
Calendar variables:							
Weekend/holiday	-0.001	-0.003	0.002	0.005	0.016	-0.010	-0.001
Quarter 2	0.015***	0.012*	-0.008	0.006	0.014	0.032***	0.018***
Quarter 3	0.008**	0.005	0.023	0.001	0.011	0.019*	0.007
Quarter 4	-0.002	-0.006	-0.007	-0.012*	0.002	0.008	0.004
Time trend 1-9	0.002**	-0.001	0.001	-0.001	-0.003	0.011***	0.001
Unemployment rate	-0.002**	-0.003*	-0.002	-0.001	0.004	0.001	-0.006***
Fast-food meal price (2011 $)	-0.007**	-0.010	-0.017	0.002	0.004	-0.018*	-0.009
Post-business cycle peak (12/07)	-0.001	0.019*	0.002	0.010	0.001	-0.057***	0.013

Notes: HH = household. Alaska and Hawaii are not included due to missing fast-food meal prices. Other variables have missing values due to "Don't know" and "Refused" responses. See appendix Table 1 for means and more discussion of missing values. For the household types single parent and couple with children, analysis excludes those age 65 and older. Excluded group is male, age 25-64, high school diploma, not employed with zero hours worked on average day, citizen, White, non-Hispanic, Northeast and metro residence, couple without children household, household income less than 200 percent of the poverty threshold, weekday day, pre-December 2007, and first quarter (January, February, March). See appendix Table 4 for coefficient estimates and model statistics. *indicates significance at the 90-percent level; **indicates significance at the 95-percent level; and ***indicates significance at the 99-percent level. Shading = not applicable.

Source: USDA, Economic Research Service estimates using American Time Use Survey and other data discussed in text.

However, the net effect (2.4 - 1.8 = 0.6) was that those who were employed and who worked up to 12 hours on the average day still had a higher probability of purchasing fast food than others.

Working more than 12 hours[20] was associated with a reduction of the marginal probability of fast-food purchase of 8.8 percentage points, one of the larger model results. Closer investigation shows that the individuals who reported working more than 12 hours were more likely to own a business or farm (30.4 percent) and were concentrated in the management, health care, or transportation fields. For these individuals, the long hours indicate that it was difficult for them to get away from their jobs, due to either the nature of the work or the isolation of the work location—so they perhaps brought their own food or had food provided for them. Although this result may seem counterintuitive, note that it is those who were employed who did not work on the average day (i.e., on their day off) that had the largest marginal probability of fast-food purchase among the labor force and work-time groups (marginal probability of employment is 0.024). This finding may suggest that the time pressure of the work week spills into days off, making fast food a desirable option.

Similar to findings in the literature, the results of this analysis show that household composition and income had a significant effect on fast-food purchasing behavior. All households with the exception of couples with children were more likely to purchase fast food than the control of couples with no children. The coefficient for number in household squared was negative as expected and significant at the 90-percent level, although the effect was very small. This finding is consistent with McCracken and Brandt (1987), who found that more people in the household increased the probability of fast-food purchase except for larger families, who had a lower probability.

Despite the bluntness of the income indicator variables, having household income greater than 200 percent above the poverty threshold for a family of four or having missing income values had positive, significant coefficients, meaning increased probability of fast-food purchase. A positive coefficient was expected for missing income value because higher income households tend to be less likely to report income.[21] This is consistent with other studies that found that higher household incomes are associated with fast-food purchase (Stewart et al., 2004; Kim and Leigh, 2011).

Personal care time, which is mostly sleep, was negatively related to fast-food purchase. An increase of an hour of personal care time was associated with a decrease in the probability of fast-food purchase of about 1 percentage point (-0.007 marginal probability). This finding is consistent with the descriptive statistics earlier. Personal care activities are considered necessary activities, and the less time spent in personal care and committed activities, the more discretionary time that an individual has. However, with the finding of fast-food purchase being associated with less sleep, it is possible that these individuals who sleep less may be so time pressured that they do not have enough time to tend to their necessary tasks so they sacrifice sleep time.[22] This finding is also consistent with other research that found less sleep is associated with poorer food choices (Buxton et al., 2009; Chaput et al., 2011; Nishiura et al., 2010).

Time spent in household tasks was negatively related to fast-food purchase, as expected. Meal preparation is part of household tasks, so by definition, fast-food purchasers would not be expected to spend as much time on meal preparation. Although the descriptive statistics showed fast-food purchasers spent slightly more time in caring for household children and adults than the total population, after controlling for other factors, time spent in caring activities does not seem to contribute to the probability of fast-food purchase. Greater travel time was associated with a greater probability of fast-food purchase as expected because of the need for individuals "on the go" to find fast and convenient food and because of the time restraints on eating typically associated with more hours of travel.[23]

Watching televison, the one recreational time variable in the model, was negatively related to fast-food purchase. This was expected because watching TV is a discretionary activity, and fast-food purchase would be more likely to occur with time-pressured individuals. However, the effect is small—an additional hour of TV watching is associated with a 0.4-percentage-point decline in the probability of fast-food purchase. Perhaps this small result reflects the dominance of television as Americans' main recreational activity.

Time spent in primary eating and drinking, the other discretionary activity variable in the model, was negative and significant—an additional hour of primary eating/drinking time is associated with a reduction of 3.4 percentage points in the probability of fast-food purchase. This is one of the larger marginal effects estimated. There is no inherent reason that actual eating/drinking time is less for a fast-food meal or snack than for other food, although there would be less waiting time to eat fast food, such as between courses at a sit-down restaurant.[24] However, this result could also indicate different eating patterns, as several studies found an association between speed of eating and energy intake, satiety, and/or body mass index (Andrade et al., 2008; Leong et al., 2011; Greene et al., 2008; Sasaki et al., 2003).

In short, although it appears that fast-food purchasers have more discretionary time than others—they spend less time sleeping, doing household tasks, and caring for others—they work more hours and spend more time traveling from place to place. They spend less time eating/drinking and are more likely to report no primary eating/drinking. It appears that fast-food purchasers are time pressed but not in a way that is easily measurable. Their time-use patterns stand out from those of other groups, and the differences suggest that fast-food purchasers have distinctly different eating patterns.

The market-level variables had mixed effects on the probability of fast-food purchase. Regional factors were not particularily strong. It is not surprising that the regional dummies are mostly insignificant because the model included the price of fast foods in each region, and previous studies used region to proxy for regional price differences (e.g., Jensen and Yen, 1996). Indeed, the analysis found that the real price of fast food was also negatively related, as expected. A dollar increase in the price (in 2011 $) of a fast-food meal was associated with a decline of about 1 percentage point of the probability of fast-food purchase, which is consistent with demand theory. The unemployment rate was negatively related to the probability of fast-food purchase, as expected. An increase in unemployment would lead to both lower household incomes for some and overall increased economic uncertainty that may curtail purchases.

Looking at behavior over the business cycle, being in the post-business cycle peak period did not seem to affect the probability of fast-food purchase. The coefficient is negative, although very small and not statistically significant. This is consistent with the visual inspection of the fast-food purchase participation rates during 2003-11 (see Figure 3), findings based on expenditure data (e.g., Okrent and Alston, 2012), and data that show sales at fast-food restaurants did not change much between 2008 and 2009 (USDA-ERS, 2013). In addition, the time trend variable is positive and significant, indicating that there may be a secular trend toward more individuals purchasing fast food on a given day. This could be due to the increased number of fast-food establishments and expanded food/beverage choices during the 2000s.

Models by Household Type

The models of fast-food purchase behavior by household type included spouse's labor force participation information as a means of proxying the household division of labor decision (Table 3). These models were estimated to account for endogeneity. The household-type marginal effects are generally the same as the "All" model in direction and significance with some exceptions. Interestingly, a woman living alone was 2.3 percentage points less likely to purchase fast food, but a woman in an "Other household with children" was 1.1 percentage points more likely to purchase fast food. The proxies for household division of labor had mixed results. For a couple with no children, the spouse being employed increased the probability of fast-food purchase of 1.7 percentage points, although not significant. For a couple with children, the only significant variable in this group is work hours vary, with a marginal effect of 5.8 percentage points, one of the larger marginal effects. This means that individuals with children and with a spouse who works varied hours had a larger probability of fast-food purchase than others. Perhaps these individuals chose fast food because of the spouse's nonstandard and irregular work hours, making it harder to plan meals.

Although the post-recession peak indicator was not significant in the "All" model, it is significant and positive in the single-person household—these individuals were 1.9 percentage points more likely to purchase fast food on the average day during or after December 2007 than before, whereas other households with no children were 5.7 percentage points less likely to purchase fast food after the business cycle peak. At the same time, these households had a positive and significant time trend, indicating that the secular upward trend of fast-food purchase mitigated the lower probability of fast-food purchase post peak. An increase in the unemployment rate was associated with a lower probability of fast-food purchase, as expected, but only for single-person households and other households with children. The remaining households did not have behavior associated with the unemployment rate.

Results of the household-type models, acknowledging the endogeneity of household decisons, support the "All" model but also reveal associations not apparent when all household types are aggregated. However, about half of individuals are in other households, typically multigenerational families. Households categorized as other are a growing segment of the U.S. population, and in 2011, over 20 percent of all U.S. households had one additional adult, frequently an adult child between ages 18 and 34 (U.S. Census, 2011). Consequently, the model results for this growing segment are relevant and not just a catchall for those who do not fit the traditional household categories.

Analysis of Pre- and Post-Business Cycle Peak

The effects of the business cycle on fast-food purchasing behavior were investigated by estimating the model for the time periods January 2003 through November 2007 and December 2007 through December 2011. First, likelihood ratio tests for structural change were conducted on a probit model using the Chow test. Chi-squared value for the probability of fast-food purchase was found to be greater than the upper tail critical value of chi-square at the 0.1 level (i.e., probability less than the critical value is 0.999), indicating a structural break in the data when evaluating 2003-07 and 2007-11. Even though figure 4 shows that the participation rates for fast-food purchase seemed unaffected by the recession and that the indicator for post-business cycle peak in the probit model of all data (Table 4) was statistically insignificant, the Chow test indicated that the slope and intercept coefficients for the period before the recession were statistically different from those during and after the recession.

Table 4 presents estimates for the two periods for all household types. Results are similar to those for the model for 2003-11, with small changes post-business cycle peak. Several of the variables have slightly smaller marginal effects for the post-peak period, reflecting the decline in jobs, income, and consumer confidence due to the recession and the recovery's soft labor market. The biggest change pre- and post-peak is for those employed—being employed added 1.5 percentage points to the probability of fast-food purchase pre-peak but added 3.4 percentage points post-peak. Perhaps those who were employed shifted expenditure from sit-down restaurants to fast food during the recession and afterward. This increase in probability of fast-food purchase by those employed seems to hold up the participation rate (see figs. 4 and 5), as many of the post-peak changes decreased the probability or increased the probability by very small amounts.

Results for the household-type models show that individuals who were single parents had a large change in behavior following the business cyle peak (BCP). For this group, the probability of purchasing fast food pre-BCP for those employed was 3.9 percentage points greater than that for those not employed but then increased to 5.2 percentage points post-BCP. Single parents' fast-food purchase was not associated with the meal's real price pre-peak, but post-peak, a $1 increase (2011$) was associated with a reduced probability of 5.1 percent.

Table 4. Selected marginal estimates at the mean based on probit model, pre- and post-BCP, by household type

	All	Single person	Single parent	Couple no children	Couple with children	Other HH, no children	Other HH with children
Labor force and HH characteristics:				Pre-BCP (January 2003 – November 2007)			
Employed	0.015***	0.007	0.039*	0.014	-0.018	0.018	0.016*
Employed part-time schedule	-0.030**	0.002	-0.076	-0.018	0.057	-0.072*	-0.026
HH income > 200% poverty thresh	0.022***	0.011	0.001	0.011	0.036*	0.025**	0.035***
HH income value missing	0.022***	0.015	0.030	-0.005	0.036	0.064***	0.022**
Time use:							
Work and work related,1-12 hours	-0.011**	0.008	-0.042*	-0.007	0.011	-0.019	-0.015*
Work and work related, >12 hours	-0.086***	-0.048**	-0.100*	-0.075***	-0.057	-0.126***	-0.090***
Primary eating/drinking, hours	-0.036***	-0.027***	-0.041***	-0.028***	-0.028***	-0.036***	-0.050***
Personal care time, hours	-0.007***	-0.005***	-0.009**	-0.006***	-0.011**	-0.009***	-0.006***
Housework, hours	-0.010***	-0.011***	-0.006	-0.009***	-0.010***	-0.010***	-0.011***

Table 4. (Continued)

	All	Single person	Single parent	Couple no children	Couple with children	Other HH, no children	Other HH with children
HH child/adult care, hours	-0.002		-0.002	-0.008	-0.006	0.014	-0.002
Watching TV, hours	-0.004***	-0.007***	-0.006*	-0.003**	-0.002	-0.006***	-0.002*
Travel time, hours	0.026***	0.022***	0.041***	0.021***	0.024***	0.022***	0.035***
Time trend 1-9	-0.003	-0.014**	0.009	-0.014*	0.006	0.002	0.005
Business cycle and price variables:							
Unemployment rate	-0.018*	-0.040**	0.035	-0.036*	0.029	-0.032	0.004
Fast-food meal price (2011 $)	-0.009*	-0.006	0.017	0.005	-0.013	-0.029*	-0.014
			Post-BCP (December 2007 – December 2011)				
Labor force characteristics:							
Employed	0.034***	0.034***	0.052**	0.021**	0.044**	0.032**	0.040***
Employed part-time schedule	0.026	-0.024	0.042	-0.002	0.061	0.046	0.043
HH income > 200% poverty threshold	0.017***	0.002	0.030	0.008	0.071***	0.028**	0.012*
HH income value missing	0.009	0.006	-0.054	-0.009	0.068**	0.033*	0.010
Time use:							
Work and work related, 1-12 hours	-0.027***	-0.004	-0.034	-0.011	-0.031	-0.033**	-0.043***
Work and work related, >12 hours	-0.089***	-0.051**	-0.198***	-0.020	-0.106	-0.115**	-0.142***
Primary eating/drinking, hours	-0.032***	-0.031***	-0.025**	-0.027***	-0.028**	-0.030***	-0.038***
Personal care time, hours	-0.007***	-0.007***	-0.008**	-0.006***	0.001	-0.009***	-0.006***

	All		Single person		Single parent		Couple no children		Couple with children		Other HH, no children		Other HH with children	
Housework, hours	-0.012	***	-0.011	***	-0.016	***	-0.012	***	-0.012	***	-0.014	***	-0.010	***
HH child/adult care, hours	0.001				0.002		0.006		-0.001		0.014		-0.002	
Watching TV, hours	-0.005	***	-0.005	***	-0.001		-0.002		-0.005		-0.005	**	-0.006	***
Travel time, hours	0.029	***	0.027	***	0.029	***	0.026	***	0.026	***	0.027	***	0.034	***
Time trend 1-9	-0.002		-0.004		0.009		-0.005		0.007		0.001		-0.002	
Business cycle and price variables:														
Unemployment rate	0.001		-0.001		-0.010		0.004		-0.002		0.006		-0.004	
Fast-food meal price (2011 $)	-0.009	*	-0.013		-0.051	**	-0.004		0.027		-0.017		-0.009	

Notes: HH = household. BCP = business cycle peak. Alaska and Hawaii are not included due to missing fast-food meal prices. Other variables have missing values due to "Don't know" and "Refused" responses. See appendix Table 1 for means and more discussion of missing values. For the household types single parent and couple with children, analysis excludes those age 65 and older. Excluded group is male, age 25- 64, high school diploma, not employed with zero hours worked on average day, citizen, White, non-Hispanic, Northeast and metro residence, couple without children household, household income less than 200 percent of the poverty threshold, weekday day, pre-December 2007, and first quarter (January, February, March).* indicates significance at the 90-percent level; ** indicates significance at the 95-percent level; and *** indicates significance at the 99-percent level.

Shading = not applicable.

Source: USDA, Economic Research Service estimates using American Time Use Survey and other data discussed in text.

Discussion

The analysis addressed questions on fast-food purchasing behavior that have not been addressed in the literature due to data limitations. Specifically, what characteristics are related to fast-food purchase? And, did fast-food purchase behavior change during or after the Great Recession?

First, findings show that Americans purchase fast food as a means of saving time. Supporting this claim, the probability of fast-food purchase is negatively correlated with time in primary eating and drinking (and, in some cases, no primary eating and drinking at all), in personal care activities (primarily sleep), and in meal preparation and was positively correlated with employment and time spent in travel from place to place.

Findings also show that the greater the number of hours a person engaged in the labor market on an average day, the less likely he or she was to purchase fast food, even after controlling for income and education. This is somewhat surprising given that McCracken and Brandt (1987), Byrne et al. (1998), Stewart and Yen (2004), and Stewart et al. (2004) found that an increased value of and hours employed in a week by the household food manager increased demand for fast food. However, previous studies used weekly hours spent in work, whereas this study used daily hours spent in work and work-related activities, and the weekly hours worked may be a proxy for whether a person was employed full-time or part-time. Hence, these previous studies might actually be picking up the positive relationship between full-time work and demand for fast food, which this study also found. Also, the previous studies do not control for time spent in leisure, travel, and household activities, which this study found to have statistically significant relationships with demand for fast food. Lastly findings show that those employed but on their day off were more likely than others to purchase fast food, indicating that the time pressure from work days spills over into nonwork days.

Second, fast-food purchasers have different eating patterns than others. They spend less time eating meals and snacks on an average day and are more likely to report no primary eating and/or drinking beverages time. Although they spend about the same amount of time in secondary eating and drinking (i.e., eating and drinking during another "main" activity), they are more likely to engage in eating while at work and while driving. To the extent that eating quickly may not be ideal, that eating/drinking activities may be so inconsequental to an individual that they are not remembered as part of the day, and that eating is done while one is engaged in activities that demand focus—work and driving—it appears that fast-food purchasers may have poor eating habits.

Third, youth and household composition (single person, single parent, and households with children) were found to have a relatively large positive and statistically significant relationship with probability of fast-food purchase. Given that average ages and household composition have changed significantly over the last several decades, these factors will become important determinants of fast-food industry growth (Stewart et al., 2004). Also, income was found to be associated with an increase in probability of fast-food purchase by 1.7 percent, which is consistent with Stewart et al. (2004), Byrne et al. (1998), and McCracken and Brandt (1987), suggesting that households with more income purchase more leisure as well as dining amenities. Note that this effect may be attributable to the bluntness of the income variable, and usage of an income variable with finer income gradients or that was continuous may lead to a more complete interpretation of the association of income and fast-food purchasing behavior over all income levels.

Fourth, fast-food purchase behavior in terms of the share of the population purchasing fast food on a given day was found to stay fairly constant during and after the Great Recession. Indeed, those employed were even more likely to purchase fast food during the recession than before the recession. Purchasing fast food has become an established part of Americans' meal and snack habits, seemingly unaffected by an economic downturn. Another plausible explanation is that the downturn fueled the demand for low-priced fast food as Americans spent less money at sit-down restaurants. This is consistent with findings that average household expenditures on fast food remained unchanged or even increased slightly during the recession (Okrent and Alston, 2012). Also, according to ERS's Food Expenditure Series (USDA-ERS, 2013), sales of meals and snacks at sit-down restaurants declined between 2008 and 2009 from $750 to $725 per capita, while sales of meals and snacks at fast-food restaurants increased from $264 to $275.

Todd (2014) found a 166-calorie per day decline from FAFH for adults age 25-64 between 2005-06 and 2009-10, with fast-food consumption accounting for just over half of this decline (84 calories). However, once the analysis controlled for demographic and employment characteristics and income, energy from FAFH was found to decline by 134 calories per day, with a little over a third of this amount attributable to fast-food consumption. This may seem contradictory to this study's finding that the rate of fast-food purchase appeared to be unaffected by the recession. However, it may be the case that individuals purchased fast food at the same frequency during the recession but were choosing items of lesser calorie content. In fact, many fast-food restaurants have started offering "healthier" menu items, especially in States and municipalities that have implemented regulations requiring provision of nutrition information at chain restaurants (e.g., Bruemmer et al., 2012). Also, Todd (2014) found evidence that between 2005-06 and 2009-10, the quality of at-home food and away-from-home food increased, partly due to individuals demanding more nutritional foods.

A better understanding of fast-food purchase behavior can inform nutrition programs and education, especially since fast food may be higher in calories and less nutritious than some other foods. To the extent that fast-food purchasers appear to be more time pressured than others, the challenge for policymakers interested in improving the dietary quality of Americans is to develop policies that make lower calorie nutritious meals fast and convenient.

REFERENCES

Aarts, H., T. Paulussen, and H. Schaalma. 1997. "Physical Exercise Habit: On the Conceptualization and Formation of Habitual Health Behaviours," *Health Education Research* 12:363-74.

Aguiar, M., E. Hurst, and L. Karabarbounis. 2013. "Time Use During the Great Recession," *American Economic Review* 103(5): 1664-1696.

Alviola, P.A., R.M. Nayga, M.R. Thompsen, D. Danforth, and J. Smartt. 2013. "The Effect of Fast-Food Restaurants on Childhood Obesity: A School Level Analysis," *Economics and Human Biology*, http://dx.doi.org/10.1016/j.ehb.2013.05.001.

Andrade, A.M., G.W. Greene, and K.J. Melanson. 2008. "Eating Slowly Led to Decreases in Energy Intake Within Meals in Healthy Women," *Journal of the American Dietetic Association* 108(7): 1186-1191.

Beatty, T.K.M., and B. Senauer. 2012. "The New Normal? U.S. Food Expenditure Patterns and the Changing Structure of Food Retailing," *American Journal of Agricultural Economics* 95(2): 318-324.

Becker, G.S. 1965. "A Theory of the Allocation of Time," *The Economic Journal* 75(299): 493-517.

Berik, G., and E. Kongar. 2013. "Time Allocation of Married Mothers and Fathers in Hard Times: The 2007-09 US Recession," *Feminist Economics*, DOI: 10.1080/13545701.2013.798425.

Bittman, M. 2002. "Social Participation and Family Welfare: The Money and Time Costs of Leisure in Australia," *Social Policy and Administration* 36(4), 408-425.

Bruemmer, B., J. Krieger, B.E. Saelens, and N. Chan. 2012. "Energy, Saturated Fat, and Sodium Were Lower in Entrées at Chain Restaurants at 18 Months Compared With 6 Months Following the Implementation of Mandatory Menu Labeling Regulation in King County, Washington," *Journal of the Academy of Nutrion and Dietetics* 112(8): 1169-76.

Burchardt, T. 2008. *Time and Income Poverty*, Case Report 57, York, UK: Centre for Analysis of Social Exclusion, www.sticerd.lse.ac.uk/dps/case/cr/CASEreport57.pdf.

Buxton, O.M., L.M. Quintiliani, M.H. Yang, C.B. Ebbeling, A.M. Stoddard, L.K. Pereira, and G. Sorensen. 2009. "Association of Sleep Adequacy With More Healthful Food Choices and Positive Workplace Experiences Among Motor Freight Workers," *American Journal of Public Health* 99 Suppl 3: S636-643.

Byrne, P.J., O. Capps, Jr., and A. Saha. 1998. "Analysis of Quick-Serve, Mid-Scale, and Up-Scale Food Away From Home Expenditures," *International Food and Agribusiness Management Review* 1(1): 51-72.

Byrne, P.J., O. Capps, Jr., and A. Saha. 1996. "Analysis of Food-Away-from-Home Expenditure Patterns for U.S. Households, 1982-89," *American Journal of Agricultural Economics* 78(3): 614-627.

Cawley, J., and F. Liu. 2012. "Maternal Employment and Childhood Obesity: A Search for Mechanisms in Time Use Data," *Economics & Human Biology* 10(4): 352-364.

Chaput, J.-P., J.-P. Després, C. Bouchard, and A. Tremblay. 2011. "The Association Between Short Sleep Duration and Weight Gain Is Dependent on Disinhibited Eating Behavior in Adults," *SLEEP* 34(10): 1291-1297.

Chen, S.E., R.J.G.M. Florax, and S.D. Snyder. 2013. "Obesity and Fast-Food Markets: A New Approach Using Geo-referenced Micro Data," *Health Economics* 22(7): 835-856.

Chou, S.-Y., M. Grossman, and H. Saffer. 2004. "An Economic Analysis of Adult Obesity: Results From the Behavioral Risk Factor Surveillance System," *Journal of Health Economics* 23(3): 565-587.

Currie, J., S. Della Vigna, E. Moretti, and V. Pathania. 2010. "The Effect of Fast Food Restaurants on Obesity and Weight Gain," *American Economic Journal: Economic Policy* 2(3): 32-63.

Dave, D.M., and I.R. Kelly. 2010. "How Does the Business Cycle Affect Eating Habits?" NBER Working Paper No. 16638, National Bureau of Economic Research, www.nber.org/papers/ w16638.

Davis, B., and C. Carpenter. 2009. "Proximity of Fast-Food Restaurants to Schools and Adolescent Obesity," *American Journal of Public Health* 99(3): 505-510.

Davis, G.C. 2013. "Food at Home Production and Consumption: Implications for Nutrition Quality and Policy," *Review of Economics of the Household*, DOI 10.1007/s11150-013-9210-0.

Dong, D., P.J. Byrne, A. Saha, O. Capps, Jr. 2000. "Determinants of Food-Away-From-Home (FAFH) Visit Frequency: A Count-Data Approach," *Journal of Restaurant & Foodservice Marketing* 4(1): 31-46.

Elliott, D.B., R. Young, and J.L. Dye. 2011. "Variation in the Formation of Complex Family Households During the Recession," Working Paper Number 2011-32, Social, Economic, and Housing Statistics Division (SEHSD), U.S. Census Bureau, http://www.census.gov/hhes/families/data/NCFR2011_Variation_in_Formation_of_Multifamily_Households_in_Recession_FINAL. pdf, tables available at http://www.census.gov/hhes/families/data/NCFR2011_Variation_in_ Formation_tables_FINAL.pdf

Federal Reserve Bank of St. Louis. 2014. "The Financial Crisis: A Timeline of Events and Policy Actions," http://timeline.stlouisfed.org/pdf/Crisis Timeline.pdf

Federal Trade Commission. 2012. *A Review of Food Marketing to Children and Adolescents*, Washington, DC.

Finlay, K.A., D. Trafimow, and A. Villarreal. 2002. "Predicting Exercise and Health Behavioral Intentions: Attitudes, Subjective Norms, and Other Behavioral Determinants," *Journal of Applied Social Psychology* 32(2): 342-358.

Greene, G.W., A. Andreade, K. Melanson, S.L. Hoerr, and K. Kattelmann. 2008. "Eating Rate and Body Mass Index in College Students," *Journal of the American Dietetic Association* 108(9): A26.

Gronau, R. 1997. "The Theory of Home Production: The Past Ten Years," *Journal of Labor Economics* 15(2): 197-205.

Gronau, R. 1986. "Home Production – A Survey," Chapter 4 (pp. 273-304) in *Handbook of Labor Economics*, O. Ashenfelter and R. Layard (eds.), Vol. 1, North-Holland: Amsterdam.

Hamermesh, D.S. 2007. "Time to Eat: Household Production Under Increasing Income Inequality," *American Journal of Agricultural Economics* 89(4): 852-863.

Hamrick, K. 2010. *Eating & Health Module User's Guide (2010) Edition,* Administrative Publication 047, U.S. Department of Agriculture, Economic Research Service, www.ers.usda.gov/ publications/ap-administrative-publication/ap-047.aspx

Hamrick, K., M. Andrews, J. Guthrie, D. Hopkins, and K. McClelland. 2011. *How Much Time Do Americans Spend on Food?* Economic Information Bulletin 86, U.S. Department of Agriculture, Economic Research Service, November, www.ers.usda.gov/publications/eib-economic-information-bulletin/eib86.aspx

Harms, T. 2014. "Reviving the USDA 1920s and 1930s Time Diary Data: A Progress Report," Presentation to Economic Research Service, June 25, 2014.

Huffman, W.E. 2011. "Household Production and the Demand for Food and Other Inputs: U.S. Evidence." *Journal of Agricultural and Resource Economics* 36(3): 465-487.

Jekanowski, M.D., J.K. Binkley, and J. Eales. 2001. "Convenience, Accessibility, and the Demand for Fast Food," *Journal of Agricultural and Resource Economics* 26(1): 58-74.

Jensen, H.H., and S.T. Yen. 1996. "Food Expenditures Away From Home by Type of Meal," *Canadian Journal of Agricultural Economics* 44: 67-80.

Kalenkoski, C.M., and K.S. Hamrick. 2013. "How Does Time Poverty Affect Behavior? A Look at Eating and Physical Activity," *Applied Economic Perspectives and Policy* 35(1): 89-105.

Kalenkoski, C.M., K.S. Hamrick, and M. Andrews. 2011. "Time Poverty Thresholds and Rates for the US Population," *Social Indicators Research* 104(1): 129-155.

Kim, D., and J.P. Leigh. 2011. "Are Meals at Full-Service and Fast-Food Restaurants "Normal" or "Inferior"?" *Population Health Management* 14(6): 307-315.

Kinsey, J. 1983. "Working Wives and the Marginal Propensity To Consume Food Away From Home," *American Journal of Agricultural Economics* 65(1): 10-19.

Kumcu, A., and A.M. Okrent. 2014. *Methodology for the Quarterly Food-Away-From-Home Prices Database*, Technical Bulletin 1938, U.S. Department of Agriculture, Economic Research Service, www.ers. usda.gov/publications/tb-technical-bulletin/tb1938.aspx

Leong, S.L., C. Madden, A. Gray, D. Waters, and C. Horwath. 2011. "Faster Self-Reported Speed of Eating Is Related to Higher Body Mass Index in a

Nationwide Survey of Middle-Aged Women," *Journal of the American Dietetic Association* 111(8): 1192-1197.

Lin, B-H., and J. Guthrie. 2012. *Nutritional Quality of Food Prepared at Home and Away From* Home, 1977-2008, Economic Information Bulletin 105, U.S. Department of Agriculture, Economic Research Service, www.ers.usda.gov/publications/eib-economic-information-bulletin/eib105.aspx

Long, J.S. 1997. *Regression Models for Categorical and Limited Dependent Variables,* Thousand Oaks, CA: Sage Publications.

McCracken, V.A., and J.A. Brandt. 1987. "Household Consumption of Food-Away-from-Home: Total Expenditure and by Type of Food Facility," *American Journal of Agricultural Economics* 69(2): 274-284.

Mincer, J. 1963. "Market Prices, Opportunity Costs, and Income Effects," in *Measurement in Economics: Studies in Mathematical Economic and Econometrics in Memory of Yehuda Grunfeld,* Stanford, CA: Stanford University Press: 67-82.

Nayga, Jr., R.M., and O. Capps, Jr. 1994. "Impact of Socio-Economic and Demographic Factors on Food Away From Home Consumption: Number of Meals and by Type of Facility," *Journal of Restaurant and Foodservice Marketing* 1: 45-69.

Neal, D., W. Wood, and J.M. Quinn. 2006. "Habits—A Repeat Performance," *Current Directions in Psychological Science* 15(4):198–202.

Nishiura, C., J. Noguchi, and H. Hashimoto. 2010. "Dietary Patterns Only Partially Explain the Effect of Short Sleep Duration on the Incidence of Obesity," *SLEEP* 33(6): 753-757.

Nord, M., M. Andrews, and S. Carlson, 2007. *Household Food Security in the United States, 2006*, Economic Research Report 49, U.S. Department of Agriculture, Economic Research Service, www.ers.usda.gov/publications/err-economic-research-report/err49.aspx

Okrent, A.M., and J.M. Alston. 2012. *The Demand for Disaggregated Food-at-Home and Food-Away-from-Home Products in the United States*, Economic Research Report 139, U.S. Department of Agriculture, Economic Research Service, www.ers.usda.gov/publications/erreconomic-research-report/err139/.aspx

Okrent, A.M., and J.M. Alston. 2011. *The Demand for Food in the United States: A Review of the Literature, Evaluation of Previous Estimates, and Presentation of New Estimates of Demand,* Monograph 48, Giannini Foundation of Agricultural Economics, Berkeley, CA, April.

Paciorek, A. 2013. "The Long and the Short of Household Formation," Finance and Economics Discussion Series Working Paper 2013-26, Federal Reserve Board, Washington, DC, April 1.

Prochaska, F.J., and R.A. Schrimper. 1973. "Opportunity Cost of Time and Other Socioeconomic Effects on Away-from-Home-Food Consumption," *American Journal of Agricultural Economics* 55(4, part 1): 595-603.

Redman, B.J. 1980. "The Impact of Women's Time Allocation on Expenditure for Meals Away from Home and Prepared Foods," *American Journal of Agricultural Economics* 62(2): 234-237.

Richards, T.J., and L. Mancino. 2013. "Demand for Food-Away-From-Home: A Multiple Discrete/ Continuous Extreme Value Model," *European Review of Agricultural Economics* doi:10.1093/ erae/jbt008.

Robinson, J.P., and G. Godbey. 1997. *Time for Life: The Surprising Ways Americans Use Their Time*, University Park, PA: The Pennsylvania State University Press.

Robinson, J.P., S. Martin, I. Glorieux, and J. Minnen. 2011. "The Overestimated Workweek Revisited," *Monthly Labor Review* 134(6): 43-53.

Sasaki, S., A. Katagiri, T. Tsuji, T. Shimoda, and K. Amano. 2003. "Self-Reported Rate of Eating Correlates With Body Mass Index in 18-Y-Old Japanese Women," *International Journal of Obesity* 27(11): 1405-1410.

Sexauer, B. 1979. "The Effect of Demographic Shifts in Changes in the Income Distribution on Food-Away-from-Home Expenditure," *American Journal of Agricultural Economics* 61(5): 1046-1057.

Soberon-Ferrer, H., and R. Dardis. 1991. "Determinants of Household Expenditures for Services," *Journal of Consumer Research* 17(4): 385-397.

Stewart, H., and S.T. Yen. 2004. "Changing Household Characteristics and the Away-From-Home Food Market: A Censored Equation System Approach," *Food Policy* 29: 643-658.

Stewart, H., N. Blisard, S. Bhuyan, and R.M. Nayga, Jr. 2004. *The Demand for Food Away From Home: Full-Service or Fast Food?* Agricultural Economic Report 829, U.S. Department of Agriculture, Economic Research Service, January, www.ers.usda.gov/publications/aer-agricultural-economic-report/aer829.aspx

Tashiro, S. 2009. "Differences in Food Preparation by Race and Ethnicity: Evidence From the American Time Use Survey," *The Review of Black Political Economy* 36(3-4): 161-180.

Todd, J. 2014. *Changes in Eating Patterns and Diet Quality Among Working-Age Adults, 2005- 2010*, Economic Research Report 161, U.S. Department of Agriculture, Economic Research Service, www.ers.usda.gov/publications/err-economic-research-report/err161.aspx

U.S. Census Bureau. 2011. "Changing American Households," presentation on C-SPAN, November 4, www.census.gov/newsroom/pdf/cah_slides.pdf

U.S. Department of Agriculture, Economic Research Service (USDA-ERS). 2013. "Food Expenditures," www.ers.usda.gov/data-products/food-expenditures.aspx

U.S. Department of Labor, Bureau of Labor Statistics (BLS). 2012. *American Time Use Survey User's Guide: Understanding ATUS 2003 to 2011*, March.

U.S. Department of Labor, Bureau of Labor Statistics (BLS). 2013a. "Consumer Price Database: All Urban Consumers (Current Series)," www.bls.gov/cpi/.

U.S. Department of Labor, Bureau of Labor Statistics (BLS). 2013b. "Employment, Hours and Earnings-State and Metro Area Database," www.bls.gov/sae/

Van Der Lippe, T., K. Tijdens, and E. de Ruijter. 2004. "Outsourcing of Domestic Tasks and Time-Saving Effects," *Journal of Family Issues* 25(2): 216-240.

Wansink, B. 2007. *Mindless Eating: Why We Eat More Than We Think*, New York: Bantam Books.

White House Task Force on Childhood Obesity Report to the President. 2010. *Solving the Problem of Childhood Obesity Within a Generation,* Executive Office of the President of the United States http://www.letsmove.gov/sites/letsmove.gov/files/TaskForce_on_Childhood_Obesity_May2010_FullReport.pdf

Wooldridge, J.M. 2002. *Econometric Analysis of Cross Section and Panel Data,* Cambridge, MA: The MIT Press.

Yen, S.T. 1993. "Working Wives and Food Away From Home: The Box-Cox Double Hurdle Model," *American Journal of Agricultural Economics* 75(4): 884-895.

Zick, C.D., and R.B. Stevens. 2009. "Trends in Americans' Food-Related Time Use: 1975-2006," *Public Health Nutrition* 13(07): 1064-1072.

Web sites

American Time Use Survey: stats.bls.gov/tus/
Eating & Health Module: ers.usda.gov/data-products/eating-and-health-module-(atus)
National Bureau of Economic Research Business Cycle page: www.nber.org/cycles/main.html

APPENDIX—DATA DEFINITIONS AND LIMITATIONS

This study used data from the 2003-11 American Time Use Survey (ATUS). The survey sample included respondents age 18 and older with "good" diaries, resulting in 117,805 respondents. "Bad" diaries are those with variable TUDQUAL2, "Collected from interviewer after interview: why do you think the data should not be used?," equal to 1 (Respondent intentionally providing wrong answer), 2 (Respondent trying to provide correct answer, but could not correctly remember his/her activities), 3 (Respondent deliberately reported very long duration activities), or 4 (Other). There were 861 of these cases. Primary eating and drinking occurrences were ATUS activities 11xxxx (ATUS major activity group "Eating and Drinking") and 050202 ("Eating and drinking as part of job, which includes eating/ drinking with clients, coworkers"). We defined **eating out** as primary eating/drinking activities that took place at restaurant or related, such that

TEWHERE = 4 (restaurant or bar),
6 (grocery store),
7 (other store/mall), or
11 (other place).

Eating/drinking at TEWHERE = 11, other place, is usually an entertainment venue when eating/ drinking is involved.[25] We include these food purchases, as concessions at movie theaters, sports venues, and other entertainment venues are essentially counter-service restaurants. We classified all other primary eating/drinking as eating/drinking elsewhere, which includes meals purchased at schools.

Diary entries were classified as **miscode** if the respondent reported primary eating/drinking at the same time as traveling[26] (i.e., activity is 11xxxx or 050202 and

TEWHERE = 12 (vehicle, driver), 13 (vehicle, passenger), 14 (walking), 15 (bus), 16 (subway/train), 17 (bicycle), 18 (boat/ferry), or 19 (taxi/limo), 20 (airplane), 21 (other mode), or 99 (unspecified mode).

It is unclear if the respondent's intention was to report primary eating/drinking while traveling, or if the interviewer recorded the activity on the wrong line. A total of 624 respondents have at least one travel miscode in their diaries, and the number of miscodes range from one to three in a diary. We reclassified these miscodes as travel time.

Because some individuals reporting **long-duration eating/drinking activities** (11xxxx and 050202) at a restaurant or related location, we identify those eating/drinking activities greater than 180 minutes (3 hours) as "events" that are likely to be catered, such as receptions. Or, because TEWHERE = 4 includes both restaurants and bars, long-duration activities could be watching sports at the bar or spending time at a nightclub. It is unlikely that these activities are regular sit-down dinners at a restaurant. For those who reported an eating activity that was over 120 minutes in their diaries, 180 minutes was the 75th percentile value. A total of 317 respondents reported eating/ drinking occasions at a restaurant (or related) of 180 minutes or more, and these cases were reassigned from eating out to primary eating/drinking elsewhere.

We identified **carryout/fast-food** purchases as activity 070103, food (not grocery) purchase that immediately follows a travel activity (180782) in the time diary. This identifies food purchased at a counter or from a delivery person where the respondent reported paying first. The examples given in the ATUS 2011 lexicon for activity 070103 are: paying the pizza delivery person, paying for meal at restaurant, paying check for a meal/drink/snack, picking up takeout food, buying fast food, placing order at a deli/fast food place, paying for fast food at drive-through, and talking to fast-food cashier/talking to the waiter. So, we excluded cases of 070103 that are paying for food or talking to a waiter at a sit-down restaurant. After the food is purchased, the individual may travel away from the restaurant (carry out the food) or may eat the food at the restaurant. Hence, we define fast-food/ carryout purchase as the sequence (1) activity 18xxxx (travel) and TEWHERE = mode of transport, and (2) activity 070103 (purchase food not groceries) and TEWHERE = 4,6,7, or 11. A total of 11,908 respondents have at least one reported carryout/fast-food purchase in their diaries over the sample period, and the number of carryout/fast-food purchases over the day range from one to six.

A number of reported eating activities at restaurants and related locations are of short duration with no reported purchase of food. We identify **short-**

duration restaurant visits as fast food if they are 20 minutes or fewer of eating/drinking (110101). Waiting time (110201) is not included in the 20-minute limit. The median time of those who purchased carryout/fast food and then reported eating/drinking within the next two activities was 20 minutes. As a consequence, we categorize restaurant visits of short duration of 20 or fewer minutes as carryout/fast food. The respondent may have neglected to report paying for the food, or the respondent may not have been the person who paid for the food. A total of 4,035 respondents reported eating at a restaurant (or related) for a duration of 20 minutes or less, and the number of such occurrences in a diary ranged from one to four. The time reported as eating/drinking at a restaurant for these short-duration restaurant visits was reassigned from eating/drinking to purchasing food (070103), and an indicator was added for fast food/carryout for these respondents. We analyzed eating/drinking times of fast-food purchasers with these short-duration eating activities classified as eating/drinking time and not fast-food purchase time, and the results do not change—fast-food purchasers still had less primary eating/drinking time and were still more likely to report no primary eating/drinking time than others. Including the short-duration restaurant eating times as primary eating/drinking activities reduces the gap between the average time spent by fast-food purchasers in eating/drinking and others, but the difference is still statistically different.

There are a number of reported **long-duration purchasing food activities** (070103). These are frequently not followed by an eating/drinking activity in the time diary. Above, we identify short-duration restaurant visits as fast food if they are 20 minutes or fewer. Here, we identify these long-duration 070103 activities as purchasing and eating/drinking food if the reported activity is more than 20 minutes. There are 458 respondents who reported purchasing carry out/fast food for durations greater than 20 minutes, with two respondents reporting two such occurrences. The time spent in these long-duration food purchasing activities was reassigned from purchasing food (070103) time to eating/drinking time (11xxxx and 050202). Although we reassigned the time, these cases were still counted as fast-food purchases.

The adjustments on short-duration restaurant eating/drinking times and long-duration food purchases are a result of the ambiguity of respondents' reporting on food purchases and consuming of these food purchases. Many of the respondents who reported a food purchase did not report eating/drinking activities within 90 minutes of the purchase. The short-duration restaurant eating/drinking activities with no food purchase reported had to include a food purchase, either by the respondent or someone else. Our goal in doing the reclassifications was to best identify fast-food purchase.

Table A.1 defines each major activity group by ATUS activity code and TEWHERE.

A time diary is a narrative—the story of a person's day. Because of the way a respondent may report his/her day, and the way in which interviewers code the reported activities, the nuances of fast-food purchase versus eating a meal at a sit-down restaurant may be lost. A respondent may not report every step of the activity and, for example, may not report paying for the food first before eating the meal at a fast-food restaurant. Or, it may be the case that the respondent was at a fast-food restaurant, but someone else paid for the meal so the respondent did not engage in the activity of purchasing food. A respondent is unlikely to report a purchase at a vending machine due to the short amount of time involved. Because of the lack of this specific information pertaining to food away from home, we made the adjustments described above. In some cases, we needed to infer the type of restaurant and specific type of activity. For example, a respondent reporting eating/drinking at a restaurant for a 10-minute duration is unlikely to be at a sit-down restaurant. Also, a respondent reporting being at a restaurant or bar from 10:00 p.m. to 2:00 a.m. is unlikely to be eating dinner and more likely to be at a bar or nightclub. There is the possibility that we inferred incorrectly in making these adjustments. In addition, we cannot tell the specific type of fast-food/carryout restaurant that the respondent visited. It could be a national chain limited-service restaurant, or it could be carryout from a sit-down restaurant. There is also the limitation that we do not know what foods or beverages the respondent ate/drank and, consequently, the caloric intake. An occurrence of fast-food purchase could be just for coffee and not a meal or snack. We also do not know how much money the respondent spent (or someone else spent) on the food/beverages. More general limitations are that the ATUS asks the respondent to report his/her primary activity only, and this may miss eating as a secondary activity. Consequently, while the data contain the purchase of fast food, they may not contain the consumption of fast food. Another possible limitation is that we use a blunt income variable to indicate if the household income is "high income"—above 200 percent of the poverty threshold. Were a continuous income variable available that was timely and consistent over 2003-11, we may have been able to better identify probabilities of fast-food purchase for various income groups before and after the business cycle peak.

A discussion of the reliability of the ATUS estimates, including sampling and nonsampling error, is in the Technical Note in each ATUS News Release.

Appendix Table 1. Time spent in various activites on an average day, 2003-11, age 18 and older

	ATUS activity codes	Total		Men		Women		Employed		Not employed		Fast-food purchasers	
Number of observations		117,805		50,751		67,054		76,451		41,354		15,122	
							Minutes						
Eating and drinking	11xxxx, 050202	67.5	[±.32]	69.6	[±.47]	65.5	[±.45]	65.9	[±.39]	70.5	[±.57]	57.2	[±.80]
Eating/ drinking out	11xxxx, 050202 and TE-WHERE= 4,6,7,11	14.1	[±.23]	14.5	[±.36]	13.7	[±.31]	14.8	[±.28]	12.7	[±.34]	16.3	[±.64]
Sit-down restaurant	as defined in text above	13.7	[±.22]	14.2	[±.35]	13.3	[±.31]	14.4	[±.27]	12.3	[±.33]	13.7	[±.61]
Fast food/ carryout	as defined in text above	0.4	[±.03]	0.3	[±.04]	0.4	[±.04]	0.3	[±.03]	0.4	[±.05]	2.6	[±.20]
Eating/ drinking elsewhere*	11xxxx, 050202 and TEWHERE not 4,6,7,11	53.4	[±.29]	55.1	[±.41]	51.7	[±.41]	51.1	[±.33]	57.7	[±.53]	40.9	[±.65]
Personal care:													
Sleep	0101xx	513.9	[±.84]	508.9	[±1.23]	518.7	[±1.12]	496.8	[±1.06]	547.4	[±1.48]	491.0	[±2.13]
Other personal care	0102xx, 0103xx, 0104xx, 0105xx, and 019999	45.9	[±.38]	38.1	[±.55]	53.2	[±.49]	45.5	[±.40]	46.6	[±.80]	46.3	[±.75]
HH activities:													
Meal prep and cleanup	0202xx	33.5	[±.30]	18.0	[±.35]	47.9	[±.47]	26.0	[±.28]	48.0	[±.70]	20.0	[±.67]
Other HH activities	all 02xxxx activities (except 0202xx, 020904)	77.8	[±.73]	65.2	[±1.03]	89.6	[±.99]	63.9	[±.75]	105.0	[±1.53]	60.5	[±1.78]

Appendix Table 1. (Continued)

	ATUS activity codes	Total		Men		Women		Employed		Not employed		Fast-food purchasers	
Caring activities:													
Caring for HH mem-bers	03xxxx	28.6	[±.39]	18.1	[±.46]	38.3	[±.57]	26.6	[±.43]	32.5	[±.80]	30.3	[±1.08]
Caring for non-HH members	04xxxx	9.7	[±.31]	8.4	[±.42]	11.0	[±.39]	7.9	[±.32]	13.4	[±.62]	11.3	[±.82]
Work, work related, and educational activities:													
Work-related activities	all 05xxxx activities except 050202	212.8	[±1.38]	255.6	[±2.18]	173.0	[±1.72]	317.5	[±1.95]	8.6**	[±.62]	241.2	[±4.55]
Educational activities purchases	06xxxx	14.1	[±.56]	12.9	[±.87]	15.1	[±.70]	11.6	[±.62]	18.9	[±1.20]	18.7	[±1.92]
Purchasing activities:													
Grocery purchases	70101	6.5	[±.11]	4.6	[±.14]	8.2	[±.16]	5.5	[±.13]	8.3	[±.25]	5.4	[±.29]
Other purchases	All 07xxxx (except 080101), 08xxxx, and 09xxxx	24.2	[±.32]	19.3	[±.48]	28.7	[±.51]	22.4	[±.33]	27.8	[±.67]	42.8	[±1.02]
Fast-food/ carryout purchases	070103, specified in text above	1.5	[±.03]	1.6	[±.05]	1.5	[±.04]	1.8	[±.04]	1.1	[±.05]	11.6	[±.13]

	ATUS activity codes	Total		Men		Women		Employed		Not employed		Fast-food purchasers	
Govern-ment, civic, religious, volunteer activities	10xxxx, 14xxxx, 15xxxx except 150101	16.8	[±.36]	14.7	[±.48]	18.9	[±.55]	14.0	[±.37]	22.5	[±.69]	18.0	[±1.17]
Leisure and sports activities:													
Watching television	120303, and 120304	162.0	[±.95]	176.3	[±1.49]	148.6	[±1.26]	128.7	[±.94]	226.8	[±2.10]	131.8	[±2.27]
Other socializing, leisure, and screentime	all 12xxxx (except 120303 and 120304), 020904, 120307, 120308, and 150101	116.8	[±.85]	115.4	[±1.36]	118.1	[±1.20]	94.2	[±.97]	160.9	[±1.79]	114.9	[±2.40]
Sports and exercise	13xxxx	17.9	[±.38]	23.3	[±.65]	12.8	[±.37]	17.7	[±.50]	18.1	[±.53]	21.6	[±1.13]
Communica-tion	16xxxx	6.3	[±.16]	3.5	[±.17]	8.8	[±.24]	4.9	[±.16]	9.0	[±.33]	7.4	[±.49]
Travel	18xxxx	74.4	[±.53]	77.2	[±.82]	71.8	[±.68]	82.1	[±.60]	59.4	[±.90]	110.7	[±1.71]
Other activities NEC	50xxxx	11.4	[±.29]	10.9	[±.46]	11.9	[±.37]	9.0	[±.32]	16.2	[±.61]	10.8	[±.89]
Total time		1440		1440		1440		1440		1440		1440	

Note: HH = household. NEC = Not elsewhere classified. 90-percent confidence intervals in brackets. Eating out is defined as primary eating/ drinking at the ATUS locations restaurant or bar, grocery store, other store/mall, and other places. Eating elsewhere is any other place. The main elsewhere locations are at home or at the workplace.

*Eating elsewhere is anywhere that is not in a restaurant.

**Work activities for those not employed are job search activities.

Appendix Table 2. Participation rates and distribution of eating behaviors, 2003-11, age 18 and older

	Total	Men	Women	Employed	Not employed	Fast-food purchasers
Participation rates (percent) and average time spent (minutes) by participants:						
% who ate out, sit-down	19.5 [±.26]	20.4 [±.41]	18.5 [±.36]	20.5 [±.33]	17.4 [±.39]	20.6 [±.75]
Ave. time spent by those who ate out, sit-down	70.6 [±.62]	69.3 [±.91]	71.9 [±.81]	70.5 [±.77]	71.0 [±.98]	66.3 [±1.62]
% who purchased fast food/carryout	13.0 [±.22]	13.5 [±.37]	12.5 [±.28]	15.2 [±.31]	8.8 [±.30]	97.9* [±.20]
Ave. time spent in purchasing FF, those who purchased FF	11.9 [±.14]	11.8 [±.20]	11.9 [±.17]	11.6 [±.16]	12.7 [±.31]	11.9 [±.14]
Distribution of eating behaviors:						
% who ate out and elsewhere	14.8 [±.23]	15.4 [±.37]	14.1 [±.31]	15.2 [±.30]	13.9 [±.34]	18.3 [±.69]
% who ate out only	5.4 [±.13]	5.7 [±.23]	5.2 [±.18]	6.0 [±.17]	4.2 [±.22]	7.5 [±.49]
% who ate elsewhere only	75.0 [±.30]	74.2 [±.43]	75.9 [±.41]	73.6 [±.35]	77.9 [±.44]	65.9 [±.89]
% who reported no primary eating/ drinking	4.8 [±.14]	4.8 [±.20]	4.9 [±.18]	5.2 [±.17]	4.0 [±.21]	8.4 [±.51]
Total	100.00	100.00	100.00	100.00	100.00	100.00

Appendix Table 3. Mean values of variables used in probit models

	N	Mean	Min value	Max-value	Standard error	90% CI	
						Min	Max
Fast-food purchase (1=FF purchase, 2=no)	117,214	1.87	1	2	0.0014	1.865	1.870
Female (1=female, 0=male)	117,214	0.52	0	1	0.0004	0.517	0.519
Age 18-24	117,214	0.12	0	1	0.0006	0.124	0.125
Age 65+	117,214	0.17	0	1	0.0002	0.165	0.165
Education, less than high school diploma	117,214	0.14	0	1	0.0013	0.134	0.139
Education, some college	117,214	0.26	0	1	0.0014	0.262	0.267
Education, college degree	117,214	0.18	0	1	0.0014	0.180	0.184
Education, advanced degree	117,214	0.10	0	1	0.0011	0.096	0.100
Employed	117,214	0.66	0	1	0.0014	0.658	0.663
Employed part-time schedule	117,214	0.02	0	1	0.0005	0.014	0.016
Noncitizen	117,214	0.08	0	1	0.0011	0.082	0.085
African-American/Black	117,214	0.12	0	1	0.0005	0.115	0.116
Asian	117,214	0.04	0	1	0.0010	0.038	0.041
Mixed race	117,214	0.01	0	1	0.0005	0.012	0.013
Hispanic	117,214	0.13	0	1	0.0004	0.131	0.132
Midwest region	117,214	0.25	0	1	0.0020	0.242	0.248
South region	117,214	0.36	0	1	0.0022	0.353	0.360

Appendix Table 3. (Continued)

	N	Mean	Min value	Max-value	Standard error	90% CI	
						Min	Max
West region	117,214	0.21	0	1	0.0018	0.212	0.218
Nonmetro residence	117,214	0.19	0	1	0.0045	0.178	0.193
Single-person household	117,214	0.15	0	1	0.0019	0.147	0.154
Single-parent household	117,214	0.03	0	1	0.0005	0.028	0.029
Couple with child(ren) household	117,214	0.05	0	1	0.0009	0.052	0.055
Other type of household, with children	117,214	0.30	0	1	0.0011	0.297	0.301
Other type of household, no children	117,214	0.21	0	1	0.0020	0.205	0.211
Number in household, squared	117,214	10.90	1	256	0.0663	10.794	11.012
Child less than age 6 in household	117,214	0.79	0	1	0.0012	0.791	0.794
Household income > 200% poverty threshold	117,214	0.54	0	1	0.0021	0.538	0.545
Household income value missing	117,214	0.12	0	1	0.0014	0.114	0.119
Work time>0 and ≤12 hours	117,214	0.45	0	1	0.0016	0.452	0.457
Work time>12 hours	117,214	0.02	0	1	0.0007	0.023	0.025
Primary eating/drinking time, hours	117,214	1.12	0	14.9	0.0033	1.119	1.130
Personal care time, hours	117,214	9.33	0	24.0	0.0092	9.316	9.346
Housework, hours	117,214	1.85	0	21.8	0.0083	1.840	1.868
Household child/adult care, hours	117,214	0.48	0	19.2	0.0040	0.469	0.482
Watching TV, hours	117,214	2.70	0	23.8	0.0097	2.686	2.717
Travel time, hours	117,214	1.24	0	24	0.0054	1.231	1.249
Weekend/holiday day	117,214	0.30	0	1	0.0005	0.297	0.298
Time trend 1-9 (2003=1,...,2011=9)	117,214	5.08	1	9	0.0017	5.073	5.079
Unemployment rate	117,214	6.65	4.4	10	0.0015	6.651	6.656
Fast-food meal price (2011 $)	117,214	3.68	2.431	5.798	0.0017	3.677	3.683

	N	Mean	Min value	Max-value	Standard error	90% CI Min	90% CI Max
Post business cycle peak (12/07)	117,214	0.47	0	1	0.0005	0.465	0.467
Quarter 2 (April, May, June)	117,214	0.25	0	1	0.0003	0.249	0.250
Quarter 3 (July, August, September)	117,214	0.25	0	1	0.0003	0.251	0.253
Quarter 4 (October, November, December)	117,214	0.25	0	1	0.0003	0.253	0.254

Appendix Table 4. Probit model coefficients, 2003-11

	All	Single person	Single parent	Couple, no children	Couple with children	Other HH, no children	Other HH with children
Intercept	-0.6713***	-0.3813**	-0.2611	-0.9271***	-1.4241***	-0.2949	-0.5006***
Demographic characteristics:							
Female	0.0059	-0.1290***	0.0997	-0.0090	0.0621	0.0292	0.0510**
Age 18-24	0.1819***	0.2029***	-0.0898	0.2070**	0.1066	0.2660***	0.1006***
Age 65+	-0.1925***	-0.1726***		-0.1010**		-0.2161***	-0.1787**
Education, less than high school	-0.0986***	-0.1216**	0.1255	-0.1323**	-0.0924	-0.0361	-0.1384***
Education, some college	0.0683***	0.0549	0.0752	0.0759**	0.0620	0.0847*	0.0386
Education, college degree	0.0776***	0.0157	0.1529**	0.1227***	0.0298	0.1166**	0.0268
Education, advanced degree	0.0242	0.0296	-0.0770	0.0028	-0.0363	0.0086	0.0496
Noncitizen	-0.3049***	-0.2150***	-0.3269**	-0.1640**	-0.3941***	-0.2893***	-0.3519***
African-American/Black	-0.0109	0.0205	-0.0469	-0.0073	0.0110	-0.0127	-0.0392
Asian	-0.1446***	-0.1843	-0.0944	-0.0224	-0.1245	-0.2942**	-0.1254**
Mixed race	0.0026	0.0556	-0.5201**	-0.0098	-0.0258	0.1234	-0.0942
Hispanic	-0.0580**	-0.0734	-0.1085	0.0402	0.0271	-0.0905	-0.0681**

Appendix Table 4. (Continued)

	All	Single person	Single parent	Couple, no children	Couple with children	Other HH, no children	Other HH with children
Geographic characteristics:							
Midwest region	-0.0132	-0.0568	-0.0317	0.0276	0.0847	-0.1149*	0.0279
South region	0.0373*	0.0598	-0.0018	0.0217	0.0823	-0.0028	0.0637**
West region	0.0277	0.0343	-0.0810	-0.0036	0.0667	-0.0069	0.0759**
Nonmetro residence	-0.0313**	-0.0200	0.0462	-0.0041	0.0699	-0.0626	-0.0475*
Labor force characteristics:							
Employed	0.1236 ***	0.1171 **	0.1910**	0.0987**	0.0582	0.1210 **	0.1244***
Employed part-time schedule	-0.0256	-0.0598	-0.1075	-0.0613	0.2944	-0.0673	0.0065
HH type:							
Single-person HH	0.0724 ***						
Single-parent HH	0.1297 ***						
Couple with child(ren) HH	0.0394						
Other type of HH, with children	0.0930 ***						
Other type of HH, no children	0.0627 ***						
HH characteristics:							
Number in HH			-0.0647		0.0732	-0.1340	-0.0261
Number in HH squared	-0.0018 *		-0.0012		-0.0084	0.0133	0.0016
Child under age 6 in HH	0.0036		-0.0138		0.0923		0.0139
Spouse employed				0.1011	-0.1501		
Spouse's usual wkly work hours				-0.0003	0.0033		
Spouse's weekly work hours vary				-0.1680	0.3183*		
HH income>200% poverty threshold	0.1009 ***	0.0385	0.0610	0.0614	0.3017***	0.1329 ***	0.1176***
HH income value missing	0.0938 ***	0.0660	0.0309	-0.0306	0.2713**	0.2681 ***	0.0802**

	All	Single person	Single parent	Couple, no children	Couple with children	Other HH, no children	Other HH with children
Time use:							
Work and work related,1-12 hrs	-0.0930 ***	0.0125	-0.1751**	-0.0510	-0.0541	-0.1231 **	-0.1268***
Work and work related, >12 hrs	-0.4501 ***	-0.2849***	-0.5989***	-0.2808**	-0.4518**	-0.5798 ***	-0.5227***
Primary eating/drinking, hours	-0.1747 ***	-0.1639***	-0.1409***	-0.1663***	-0.1570***	-0.1592 ***	-0.2079***
Personal care time, hours	-0.0349 ***	-0.0333***	-0.0377***	-0.0358***	-0.0323*	-0.0448 ***	-0.0268***
Housework, hours	-0.0561 ***	-0.0624***	-0.0492***	-0.0601***	-0.0616***	-0.0578 ***	-0.0498***
HH child/adult care, hours	-0.0019		-0.0006	-0.0033	-0.0182	0.0658 **	-0.0095
Watching TV, hours	-0.0233 ***	-0.0318***	-0.0144	-0.0164***	-0.0194	-0.0270 ***	-0.0209***
Travel time, hours	0.1406 ***	0.1351***	0.1569***	0.1381***	0.1415***	0.1215 ***	0.1614***
Calendar variables:							
Weekend/holiday	-0.0048	-0.0185	0.0074	0.0306	0.0865	-0.0488	-0.0049
Quarter 2	0.0793***	0.0662*	-0.0376	0.0384	0.0763	0.1542***	0.0829***
Quarter 3	0.0432**	0.0305	0.1024	0.0054	0.0615	0.0936*	0.0348
Quarter 4	-0.0102	-0.0359	-0.0317	-0.0703*	0.0103	0.0408	0.0162
Time trend 1-9	0.0115**	-0.0021	0.0021	-0.0012	-0.0166	0.0536***	0.0040
Unemployment rate	-0.0118**	-0.0188*	-0.0112	-0.0022	0.0225	0.0019	-0.0264***
Fast-food meal price (2011 $)	-0.0365**	-0.0563	-0.0735	0.0125	0.0195	-0.0854*	-0.0413
Post-business cycle peak (12/07)	-0.0066	0.1044*	0.0080	0.0594	0.0050	-0.2784***	0.0626

Appendix Table 4. (Continued)

	All	Single person	Single parent	Couple, no children	Couple with children	Other HH, no children	Other HH with children
Number of observations	117,214	28,380	6,938	22,978	5,044	13,206	40,615
Percent of observations that are fast-food purchasers	12.8	11.1	16.0	10.4	13.0	12.8	14.9
Likelihood ratio, Pr>ChiSq	<.0001	<.0001	<.0001	<.0001	<.0001	<.0001	<.0001
Score, Pr>ChiSq	<.0001	<.0001	<.0001	<.0001	<.0001	<.0001	<.0001
Wald, Pr>ChiSq	<.0001	<.0001	<.0001	<.0001	<.0001	<.0001	<.0001
Association of predicted and observed:							
Concordant	70.2	71.3	67.3	70.5	67.9	71.2	69.3
Discordant	29.1	28.0	32.0	28.7	31.4	28.2	30.0
Tied	0.7	0.7	0.7	0.8	0.7	0.6	0.7

Notes: HH = household. Alaska and Hawaii are not included due to missing fast-food meal prices. Other variables have missing values due to “Don’t know” and “Refused” responses. See appendix Table 3 for means and more discussion of missing values. For the household types single parent and couple with children, analysis excludes those age 65 and older. Excluded group is male, age 25-64, high school diploma, not employed with zero hours worked on average day, citizen, White, non-Hispanic, Northeast and metro residence, couple without children household, household income less than 200 percent of the poverty threshold, weekday day, pre-December 2007, and first quarter (January, February, March). * indicates significance at the 90-percent level; ** indicates significance at the 95-percent level; and *** indicates significance at the 99-percent level. Shading = not applicable.

Source: USDA, Economic Research Service estimates using American Time Use Survey and other data discussed in text.

End Notes

[1] According to Byrne et al. (1998), upscale restaurants offer full alcohol service and accept credit cards whereas mid-scale restaurants do not.

[2] See the National Bureau of Economic Research, US Business Cycle Expansions and Contractions, http://www.nber.org/cycles/cyclesmain.html

[3] One potential drawback of the ATUS diary data is that information on only 1 time-diary day per person was collected. There may be concern that some activities, such as eating fast food or engaging in sports and exercise, are not daily activities and, thus, a 1-day diary lacks intrapersonal variability. However, some activities, such as eating patterns, have a large degree of persistency, meaning that day-to-day variation is minimal. Wansink (2007) discusses the myriad external influences that result in eating habits. Exercise is also considered to be a habit, and researchers have studied what contributes to habitual exercise (Aarts et al., 1997; Finlay et al., 2002). Indeed, much of an individual's daily activities can be classified as habitual repetition (Neal et. al., 2006). Another argument for using the ATUS 1-day time diary data is that the ATUS is large and nationally representative, and so intrapersonal variability would not be an issue.

[4] Supplemental analysis was done using the 2006-08 ATUS Eating & Health Module (EHM). The pooled 2006-08 microdata files contain 37,832 completed interviews. The EHM Respondent and Replicate weights files were used. Estimation procedures outlined in the EHM User's Guide (Hamrick, 2010) were followed.

[5] Totals do not always add up exactly due to rounding, and may be off by ±0.1 minute or ±0.1 percentage point.

[6] Fast-food purchasers spent, on average, 3.0 minutes in sleeplessness and 488.0 minutes actually sleeping, for a total of 491.0 minutes. The total population spent, on average, 3.5 minutes in sleeplessness and 510.5 minutes actually sleeping, totaling 513.9 minutes.

[7] The rate of household formation—people setting up new households—dropped considerably over 2007-11 as families and unrelated individuals "doubled up" in the same household (Elliott et al., 2011; Paciorek, 2013).

[8] We also analyzed data for the time periods January 2003-November 2007, December 2007-June 2009, and July 2009-December 2011 and found little difference between time-use patterns for December 2007-June 2009 and for July 2009-December 2011. This is likely due to the soft labor market during the recovery.

[9] We considered modeling demand for fast food as hurdle model such that the hurdle would be the probability of purchasing fast food, and then the second model would be predicting the time spent in purchasing and/or eating fast food conditional upon fast-food purchase. However, since the distribution of the time duration of purchasing fast food is fairly narrow, and the time spent eating fast food is not straightforward, we concluded that a double-hurdle model would not be useful. First, almost half of fast-food purchasers do not report eating fast food as a primary activity within 90 minutes of purchasing fast food, and those that do report eating fast food typically do so in a small window of time (between 15 and 30 minutes). Looking at the 2006-08 ATUS Eating & Health Module data, which included data on secondary eating and drinking (i.e., eating/drinking while doing something else), we found that of those who reported no primary eating/ drinking time after fast-food purchase, only 22.5 percent reported secondary eating and only 9 percent reported secondary drinking after fast-food purchase. Consequently, we concluded that estimating the amount of time spent eating/drinking fast food would be difficult, likely to contain measurement error, and

not particularly revealing because fast-food purchasers reported relatively short durations of eating/drinking occurrences, if any at all.

[10] Results show 85.3 percent of fast-food purchasers had only 1 purchase, 13.0 percent had 2 purchases, 1.4 percent had 3 purchases, and the remainder had 4-6 purchases. As a robustness check, we also modeled the number of fast-food purchases within a day by an individual as a zero-inflated Poisson model. The results of the zero-inflated Poisson models were consistent with the findings presented in this study.

[11] Wooldridge (2002) stated that "Putting in the averages for the binary variables means that the effect does not really correspond to a particular individual. But often the results are similar, and the choice is really based on taste" (p. 466).

[12] See Bittman (2002) and Burchardt (2008).

[13] Looking at total population (age 15 and older) averages, watching television has been the third-longest duration activity each year since the ATUS started. For 2011, sleeping was the longest duration activity at 8.71 hours on an average day, paid work was 3.20 hours, and watching television was 2.75 hours. Watching television dominates the combined major categories of leisure and sports, which have an average time of 5.21 hours on an average day. The next-longest duration activity was eating and drinking, at 1.24 hours (U.S. Bureau of Labor Statistics, American Time Use Survey—2011 Results News Release, USDL-12-1246, June 22, 2012).

[14] We performed the Smith-Blundell endogeneity test on time spent in household activities (including meal production time) for our probit model of fast-food purchase. The instrument used was female (=1 if respondent was female). Based on this test, we could not reject the null hypothesis that the model is specified properly and, hence, concluded endogeneity was not a problem.

[15] These categories are based on the ATUS respondent and not the totality of the household, as we have information only on the individual who did or did not purchase fast food. The "other household" categories occur because of this focus on the respondent. For example, a household with a married couple with two children, one age 20 and the other age 15, would have different categorizations depending on which family member was the respondent. If either parent was the respondent, then the category would be "married couple with children." If either of the children was the respondent, then the category would be "other household with children." Another example is a household that included just a married couple and a child age 20. If either parent was the respondent, then the household category would be "married couple without children" (because the child is age 18 or older), or if the 20-year-old child was the respondent then the household category would be "other household without children."

[16] See Davis (2013) for a comprehensive review.

[17] We also tried the ratio of the price of limited-service meals to the price of full-service meals, but that variable was not successful. In some Census divisions, the prices would move in lockstep, resulting in a constant ratio over the time period; in other divisions, the ratio varied considerably. With both these price patterns in the same variable, the net result was that the ratio variable was not significant.

[18] The income survey question—household income over the previous 12 months—was asked of the respondent's household in the first month of the Current Population Survey, which would have been 18-21 months before the ATUS interview. In addition, the CPS income variable has a large amount of nonresponse, which is why we included an "income value missing" variable in the model. To complicate the variable, imputation of missing income

values began in January 2010. These income imputations start appearing in the ATUS in March 2010.

[19] The "All" model and the household-type models include gender as an independent variable. We did not find evidence in either the descriptive statistics or the multivariate analysis to warrant dividing our analysis into more detailed subgroups, such as estimating the household-type models by gender.

[20] We analyzed the behavior for paid work hour by hour to determine whether a break point existed and found that the time-use patterns were noticeably different for those with more than 12 hours of paid work versus those with 1-12 hours of paid work.

[21] The authors' analysis of missing income observations in the Current Population Survey Food Security Supplement found that the prevalence of food insecurity of the unknown income group was about the same as that for households with income 185 percent of the poverty threshold (Nord et al., 2007). Indeed, for other measures of food security in the report, the estimates of the missing income group were similar to those for households with income 185 percent of the poverty threshold. The authors concluded that the households with missing income were disproportionately households with income above 185 percent of the poverty threshold.

[22] In a variation of the model presented, we included a variable for time poverty of the individual (not shown) and found that time poverty was associated with a lower probability of fast-food purchase, which is consistent with Kalenkoski and Hamrick (2013). In this analysis, we explore the components of time poverty and their association with fast-food purchase because we speculated that fast-food purchasers may be time pressured in a way that is not captured by a time-poverty threshold. Time-poor individuals have shorter average sleep time than the total population, which may be the result of time pressure and appears to give these individuals more discretionary time. In particular, fast-food purchasers had an average total discretionary time of 516.0 minutes, compared with 498.1 minutes for the total population, and the difference, 17.9 minutes, is similar to the difference between the average sleep time for fast-food purchasers (491.0 minutes) and that for the total population (513.9 minutes).

[23] Using the 2006-08 ATUS Eating & Health Module data, we found that fast-food purchasers were more likely to engage in secondary eating or secondary drinking while driving a vehicle than other individuals.

[24] Waiting to eat time (activities 1102xx) is infrequently reported in the ATUS diaries. Fast-food purchasers and those who ate at sit-down restaurants both reported average "waiting associated with eating time" as less than 1 minute. It is likely that respondents instead report their wait time as socializing, grooming (restroom visit), reading, or cell phone use.

[25] Secondary eating and secondary drinking (survey questions in the 2006-08 ATUS Eating & Health Module) that were coded as "Other place" mostly took place at a stadium, arena, ball field, or a movie theater. Personal correspondence with Dorinda Allard, U.S. Bureau of Labor Statistics, and Jennifer Montcalm, U.S. Census Bureau, via email on February 28 and 29, 2008.

[26] Email correspondence with Rachel Krantz-Kent dated May 16, 2014, and ATUS Coding Rules 2011, version 05/28/08, Miscellaneous rule #6.

In: Purchasing Food Away from Home
Editor: Rebecca Evans
ISBN: 978-1-63483-728-6

Chapter 2

The Demand for Food Away from Home: Full Service or Fast Food?

Hayden Stewart, Noel Blisard, Sanjib Bhyuan and Rodolfo M. Nayga, Jr.*

Abstract

Consumer spending at full-service and fast food restaurants will continue to grow over the remainder of this decade and the next. However, the larger increase is predicted to occur at full-service restaurants. Simulations assuming modest growth in household income plus expected demographic developments show that per capita spending could rise by 18 percent at full-service restaurants and by 6 percent for fast food between 2000 and 2020. The assumed increase in income alone causes such spending to rise by almost 15 percent and 7 percent at full-service and fast food restaurants, respectively. The increasing proportion of households containing a single person or multiple adults without live-at-home children will cause per person spending to rise by another 1 to 2 percent in each of these segments. However, the aging of the population will decrease spending on fast food by about 2 percent per capita.

* SanjibBhuyan is a member of the faculty at the Department of Agricultural, Food, and Resource Economics at Rutgers University. Rodolfo M. Nayga, Jr., is a member of the faculty at the Department of Agricultural Economics at Texas A&M University.

Keywords: Full-service restaurants, fast food restaurants, food spending, household income

SUMMARY

Consumer spending at full-service and fast food restaurants will continue to grow over the remainder of this decade and the next. However, the larger increase will likely occur at full-service restaurants. Simulations assuming modest growth in household income plus expected demographic developments show that per capita spending could rise by 18 percent at full-service restaurants and by 6 percent for fast food between 2000 and 2020. The assumed increase in income alone causes such spending to rise by almost 15 percent and 7 percent at full-service and fast food restaurants, respectively. The increasing proportion of households containing a single person or multiple adults without live-at-home children will cause per person spending to rise by another 1 to 2 percent in each of these segments. However, the aging of the population will decrease per person spending on fast food by about 2 percent per capita.

Fast food restaurants had been increasing their share of the growing away-from-home market until the middle of the 1990s. Sales at fast food restaurants briefly surpassed those at full-service restaurants around the same time. However, the fast food share of the away-from-home market has been relatively steady since then. In 2002, full-service restaurants again accounted for a slightly larger share of total sales.

A household's demand for food away from home depends on its income as well as on its demographics. A 10-percent increase in a typical household's per capita income would cause it to spend 6.4 percent and 3.2 percent more per capita at full-service and fast food restaurants, respectively. Away-from-home expenditures are typically higher for single-person households and households containing multiple adults without live-at-home children. For instance, a single person spends almost $3 more per person each week at each type of establishment than an otherwise identical person who is married and has live-at-home children.

Current and future changes in the away-from-home market could reflect changes in the diet and health of American consumers. Any shift in market share between fast food and full-service restaurants may reflect important changes in what people are eating away from home, because fast food tends to have different quantities of fat and calories than meals prepared at full-service restaurants.

This study also represents a necessary first step in understanding how and why the structure of the foodservice industry is changing. As the demand for meals and snacks at full-service restaurants increases relative to the demand for fast food, restaurant companies will be motivated to adjust what menu items and services they offer. To be sure, such adjustments might also alter any projected changes in market share between full-service and fast food establishments.

INTRODUCTION

Americans now spend nearly half of their food dollars on meals and snacks at foodservice facilities, such as restaurants, hotels, and schools. Total away-from-home expenditures, defined to include all food dispensed for immediate consumption outside of the consumer's home, amounted to $415 billion in 2002.[1] That is about 58 percent greater than annual away-from-home expenditures in 1992 which totaled $263 billion. Even after accounting for inflation and business cycles (Figure 1), expenditures still increased by 23 percent between 1992 and 2002. We anticipate that households will continue to increase their spending on foodservice meals and snacks at an annual rate of about 1.2 percent in real (inflation-adjusted) terms (Blisard et al., 2003).[2] Rising household incomes and demographic developments, such as smaller household sizes, will account for this. However, it is not clear what types of foodservice facilities will be selling these meals and snacks.

A diverse array of foodservice firms—full-service restaurants, fast food establishments, hotels, retail stores, recreation places, bars, and operators of vending machines—compete for the consumer's away-from-home dollar. However, full-service and fast food restaurants have captured the bulk of the market, with 39.9 percent and 37.9 percent of total sales in 2002 (Figure 2).[3] Full-service restaurants, defined as establishments with waitstaff, tend to offer more varied menus and dining amenities. Fast food establishments tend to emphasize convenience (Table 1).

The composition of the away-from-home market is dynamic. The full-service and fast food segments now command a similar share of the market, but it is unclear which segment is poised to expand relative to the other. Until the middle of the 1990s, sales of fast food were increasing faster, and briefly surpassed those at full-service restaurants. This upsurge was buoyed by the strategic location of new fast food outlets. Convenience is a major sales point for fast food operators. If driving to an outlet takes longer than cooking at home, then fast food is not truly convenient.[4] Thus, as fast food companies open more outlets per square mile in appropriate locations, consumers have to travel less for fast food, on average. In turn, these new store openings have stimulated the demand for fast food (Jekanowski et al., 2001). The proliferation of fast food restaurants can be seen in a trend known as "channel-blurring," whereby gas stations and retail stores, such as Wal-Mart and Target, are hosting foodservice chains like Pizza Hut and Taco Bell.

The relative expansion of the fast food market segment appears to have stalled in recent years. In 2002, sales at full-service restaurants accounted for a slightly larger share of total away-from-home spending, while, in 2003, McDonald's reduced its estimates for near-term sales growth from 15 percent to 2 percent (Gogoi and Arndt, 2003). Meanwhile, Burger King was sold to a group of investors in December 2002 for $1.5 billion. Five months earlier, these same investors had offered $2.26 billion for the company. Reasons cited by the investors for scaling back their offer included the competitive environment in which Burger King and other fast food chains now operate.

The full-service restaurant segment is seemingly poised to expand its share of the away-from-home market (*Restaurant Industry 2010: The Road Ahead*).[5] The National Restaurant Association believes that the overall growth of the market will depend on rising incomes and demographic changes. However, it also argues that these demand forces will have the greatestimpact on the kinds of services and types of menus typically available at full-service restaurants.

Table 1. Segments of the Market at a Glance

Item	Full-service	Fast food
Share of sales in2002 (percent)[1]	39.9	37.9
Number of outlets[2]	191, 245	214, 774
Number of paidemployees (million)[2]	3.6	3.3
Sales points and diningamenities	Variety	Convenience

[1] CPI, Prices, and Expenditures: Expenditure Tables. USDA/ERS. The remainder, 22.2 percent, is for sales at hotels/motels, schools and colleges, retail stores, recreational places, and other foodservice establishments.

[2] 1997 Economic Census. Accommodation and Foodservice. Bureau of the Census.

Any shift in market share between fast food and full-service restaurants may further affect what foods and services restaurants of both types offer. If trends in demand favor full-service restaurants, the market could soon include more full-service restaurants offering more varied menus and a wider range of dining amenities. Fast food restaurants might also introduce many of these same foods and services themselves.

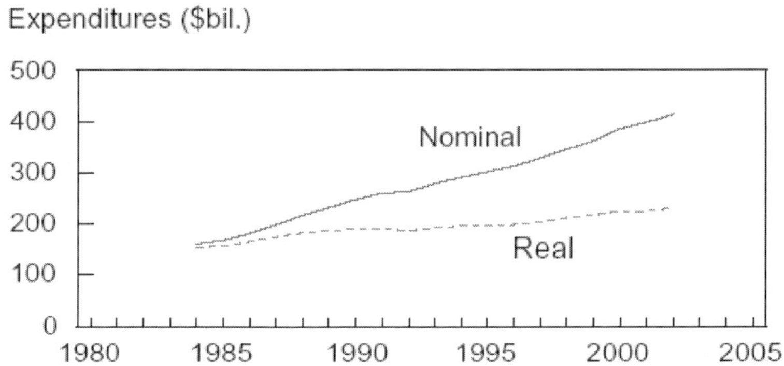

Source:Food CPI, Prices, and Expenditures: Expenditure Tables. Economic Research Service.

Figure 1. Annual away-from-home expendituresExpenditures ($bil.)

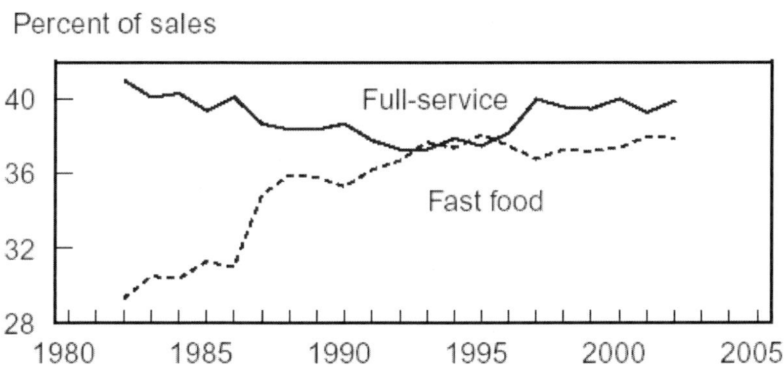

Source:Food CPI, Prices, and Expenditures: Expenditure Tables. Economic Research Service.

Figure 2. The away-from-home market by outlet type.

Developments in the demand for foodservice meals and snacks could also reflect important changes in the diet and health of the American population. Fast food tends to have different quantities of fat and calories than meals prepared at full-service restaurants (Lin and Frazao, 1999). Thus, to the extent that any shift in expenditures reflects changes in consumption, it is likely that changes also are occurring in the healthfulness of what consumers are eating away from home.

This study examines how the demand for food away from home is changing, how these changes could affect the size of the full-service and fast food segments, and the implications for how restaurants might respond. In particular, we focus on how developments in the economic and demographic characteristics of the Nation's population may be leading to changes in demand for the foods and services supplied by restaurants. Important trends in the U.S. population include rising incomes, an aging population, smaller household sizes, and an increasingly high proportion of households containing single people or multiple adults without live-at-home children. These developments could prompt changes in the demand for food away from home that will affect both the supply of restaurant foods and services as well as the diet and health of the consumers who demand those items.

DETERMINANTS OF CONSUMER DEMAND

The theory of household production, outlined by Becker (1965), extends classical demand theory to consider how prices, income, demographics, and time constraints can all influence a household's purchases of items like food. This economic model of household behavior holds that the costs of consumption can include prices as well as time spent eating food, preparing food, and cleaning up after a meal or snack. A household must therefore decide whether to spend time on all aspects of the activity of eating a meal (i.e., prepare food at home) or outsource some aspects like preparation and cleaning up (i.e., purchase food away from home). The optimal decision depends on many factors, including the household's finances, the opportunity cost of its manager's time, and how well the household manager can cook. In the context of Becker's model, a household manager can be defined as the person primarily responsible for shopping, cooking, cleaning, and other household chores.

Empirical analyses have further shown how specific economic and demographic characteristics of a household can influence its demand for food away from home by market segment. Four such studies use household survey data from the 1970s and 1980s. McCracken and Brandt (1987) and Byrne et al. (1998), analyzed the relationship between some key household characteristics and expenditures at each type of restaurant. Nayga and Capps (1994) studied the relationship between a household's characteristics and its frequency of dining at each type of facility. Also, Hiemstra and Kim (1995) analyzed the impact of household characteristics on expenditure by eating occasion and market segment.[6] Characteristics found to be important in these studies include the household's income, time constraints faced by the household manager, the household manager's age, number of people in the household, education level of the household manager, the household's region of residence, and the household's race and ethnicity.

Households with higher incomes tend to spend more on products and services, including leisure, variety, and dining amenities like waitstaff, ambience, and alcohol service. Food away from home is a form ofleisure where leisure is defined as time spent outside of both the labor force and household production. Both fast food and full-service restaurants can provide leisure for a household manager who is freed from cooking, cleaning, and shopping. Moreover, along with the additional leisure, households with more income may also buy more variety and other dining amenities. Thus, households with higher incomes have been shown to have higher expenditures for both fast food and full-service meals and snacks, but spending at full-service restaurants is most responsive to any changes in income (e.g., McCracken and Brandt, 1987; Byrne et al., 1998).

Households also may demand more food away from home as their manager works longer hours outside the home. In particular, fast food may come to represent a convenient meal option, if such a restaurant is reasonably accessible. Spending for fast food has been shown to increase along with the number of hours worked by a household manager in the labor force (e.g., Byrne et al., 1998). By contrast, dining at a full-service restaurant can take as long as preparing, eating, and cleaning up after a meal at home. Thus, there is neither a clear theoretical nor empirical relationship between a household's demand for food at full-service restaurants and its time constraints.

The number of people living in a household also may influence its demand for meals and snacks away from home. In particular, as a household adds more members, food prepared at home may become more economical. For example, it might take 20 minutes to prepare a meal for one person at home, but just 30 minutes to prepare a meal for four people. When cooking at home, the household with more members can also benefit by purchasing larger package sizes with lower per unit costs. In total, single-person households will likely have the highest time and monetary costs per person for eating at home, while larger households will incur lower costs per capita. Empirical studies do find that larger households tend to spend less money per capita away from home (e.g., McCracken and Brandt, 1987).

A household's demand for food away from home also may depend on the ages of its members. One reason is that tastes may change as people age. For example, if the sensitivity of taste buds diminishes with age, older people may demand foods with bolder flavors (Friddle et al., 2001). Also, older and younger people may have different opportunities to socialize, so if theyeat out for different reasons, they may logically go to different kinds of establishments. On balance, empirical studies find that households with younger members tend to spend more money on fast food, while households with older people tend to spend more money on full-service dining (Byrne et al., 1998).

The impact of aging on demand is complicated by uncertainty about whether generations will retain their distinctive eating habits as they age. For example, will an elderly person in 2020 have the same expenditure patterns as an elderly person now with similar characteristics? Perhaps not. Younger generations know less about cooking than earlier generations did at the same point in their life (Foodservice 2010). However, even if this argument is true, younger generations may still evolve like older generations. Younger generations may compensate for their lack of skills by taking advantage of the growing array of prepared foods and convenience appliances. In fact, Blisard (2001) finds that members of different generations tend to have similar behavior away from home at the same points in their lives.

Does the structure of a household also influence its demand for meals and snacks away from home? For instance, a married couple with children is likely to have different preferences and preparation capabilities than a single-parent family, a single-person household, and multiple adults living together without children. Even after controlling for hours worked in the labor force and income, members of each of these types of household may not share the same opportunities to socialize or face the same time constraints. This is a subject area not taken up by previous research.

Effect of Household Characteristics on Demand

Our first step in this analysis is to identify the characteristics of a household that are potential determinants of its demand for food away from home. In addition to characteristics identified in past studies, we include the structure of a household, whether it is comprised of a married couple with children, a single parent with children, a single person, or multiple adults without live-at-home children. A data set must also be identified to empirically examine the relationships between the characteristics of a household and that household's demand for meals and snacks at both fast food and full-service restaurants.

Changing Structure of Households

The increasing incidence of alternative types of household in the U.S. has been much publicized (e.g., Kinsey, 1990). In this study, we define a traditional household as a married couple with live-at-home children. Traditional households accounted for 30.2 percent of all households in 1980, but just 23.5 percent in 2000 (Cromartie, 2002). Single-person households, single-parent families, and households of multiple adults without a live-at-home child are on the rise (see box, "Changing Structure of American Households").

Changing Structure of American Households

The structure of the American household is changing. The average age is higher, people are better educated, and there are fewer members per households. More Americans are also living outside of a traditional family (a married couple with live-at-home children).

A household's structure can have significant implications for how it buys and prepares food. For example, families with three or more children are considered a prime market for the basic food ingredients and volume discounts traditionally provided by grocery stores (Kinsey, 1990).

Demographic changes are behind the increasing frequency of nontraditional households. There are more "empty nest" adults living together after their children have grown up, as well as more unmarried people who are perhaps waiting longer to get married or who have been widowed (Cromartie, 2002).

This report seeks to determine whether nontraditional households eat out more or less often than their traditional counterparts, and where they tend to spend their money. For example, as compared with a married couple engaged in child rearing, single people may have more social opportunities to dine out at full-service restaurants.

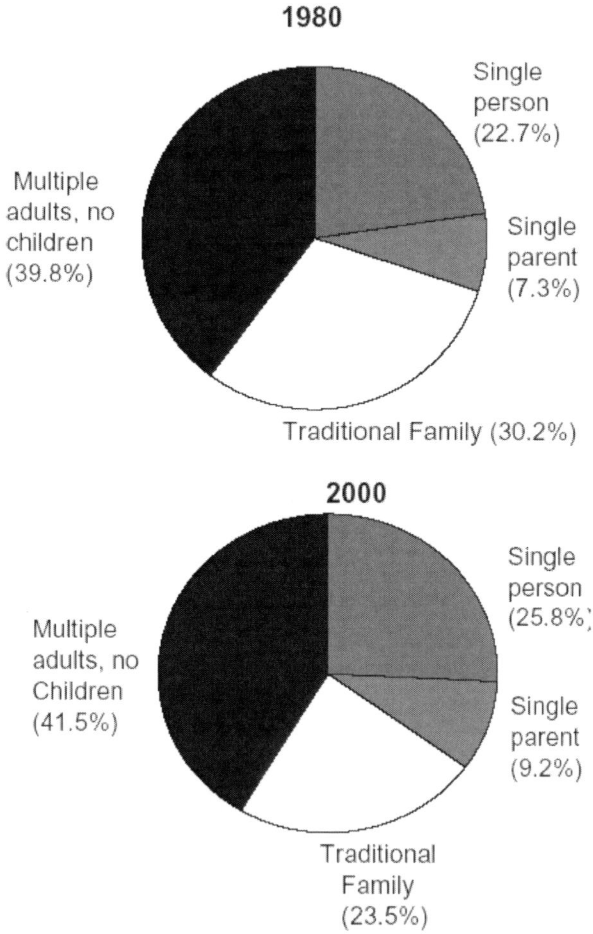

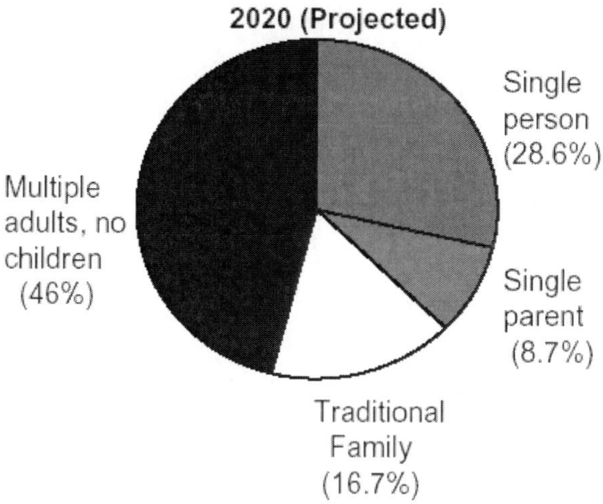

Source: Derived from Cromartie, 2002, who provides projections for traditional, single-person, and single-parent households. He also provides a projection for married couples without children. However, these four categories are not all encompassing. Some household types do not belong to any group, e.g., unmarried, cohabitating adults without children. Thus, in this study, we derived projections for households comprised of multiple adults without children by determining the percentage of households not belonging to any one of the other three groups. It follows that this fourth group includes all households with multiple adults and no children.

Differences are likely to exist in the preferences and household production capabilities of diverse types of households. Members of single-person households may be more likely to socialize and date than members of a traditional family. But do these pursuits inflate one's expenditures at full-service or fast food establishments? For example, dating might lend itself to full-service restaurants promising a leisurely dining experience, while fast food establishments with play facilities may appeal more to families with children.

Single-parent households also may differ from traditional households in that they are more likely to contend with limited social opportunities, financial insecurity, and greater time constraints. These factors could influence a single-parent household's demand for convenience or other amenities associated with dining away from home.

A household with multiple adults and no child rearing responsibilities could also be very different. Having no children to raise could increase the household's ability to finance dining away from home, and expand its set of social opportunities. Greater financial resources and fewer time constraints might encourage the household to spend more money at full-service restaurants in particular.

Data Used in the Analysis

To test hypotheses about how a household's demand for food away from home is affected by its structure and other characteristics, we need a data set with information on households, their characteristics, and how much they spend in each market segment. The ideal set of data for this study would include information on at least several thousand households, the characteristics of each household, and how much eachhousehold spent in each market segment. Moreover, it would follow this sample of households over 20 to 50 years, and report on how each household's characteristics and expenditures have changed. By witnessing how each household's food spending changed with its characteristics, we might project how spending is likely to further evolve as each current household becomes wealthier, older, or different in structure. Unfortunately, these data are not available. Still, employing some assumptions, we can adapt existing sources of data to undertake the same sort of analysis.

The Bureau of Labor Statistics (BLS) provides the only public survey of household characteristics and household expenditures.[7] The BLS Consumer Expenditure Survey (CES) is an annual representative sample of spending by American households.[8] In the diary section of the survey, each household reports its expenditures on food away from home and other goods for 2 weeks. These data can also be matched with information about each household, such as its income, number of members, region, and race.

The CES does not follow the same households over time, and it does not classify household expenditures away from home prior to 1998. The BLS surveys a household for one 2-week period, and then drops this household from its survey. Thus, each annual survey contains a completely different set of households. Moreover, because the BLS did not break down away-from-home spending on fast food versus food at full-service restaurants prior to 1998, we can only use data on household characteristics and their spending patterns for 1998, 1999, and 2000.[9]

An additional limitation of household surveys in general, including the CES, is that they do not includeexpenditures by businesses or for people in institutions. It follows that the analysis in this study does not capture all of the away-from-home market. In order to determine how much of the market is captured by the CES, we undertook a "back of the envelope" calculation. In

2000, among house-holds completing the survey, we find that per capita away-from-home spending averaged \$19.21 each week, not including alcohol. It follows that households in the United States spent about \$1, 000 per person per year. Thus, since the U.S. population equaled 281 million in 2000, it can be further estimated that spending by all households was around \$281 billion. We estimate that the CES captures about 75 percent of the total market, since the size of the away-from-home market was approximately \$385 billion in 2000 (Figure 1).

STATISTICAL MODEL OF AWAY-FROM-HOME EXPENDITURES

The statistical model used in this report relates a household's pattern of spending away from home to its economic and demographic characteristics, but not to prices. We recognize that prices are an important determinant of demand. However, since the CES does not contain information on prices and our data were collected over a short period of time, we assume that there was little variation in the price of fast food relative to the price of food at full-service restaurants over the period when the data were collected. In other words, households are assumed to have faced similar relative prices.[10] This assumption allows us to view a household's expenditures on meals and snacks as value-weighted quantities. For example, a meal at a full-service restaurant may be more costly than a meal at a fast food restaurant. It is therefore possible that a household eats fast food more often than full-service meals, but reports similar expenditures in both market segments. In this case, price differences serve toweight the value of purchases to the household. In fact, a similarity of expenditures in the two segments would suggest that the household receives similar levels of satisfaction from its total purchases of both types of food away from home. Viewing prices as weights for aggregating purchases in this way is consistent with classical demand theory (Green, 1964).

The Statistical Model

The statistical model will provide more accurate estimates of the relationships between a household's characteristics and its spending away from home, if we simultaneously estimate the equations for spending on fast food and spending at full-service restaurants. For instance, because of variation in how much household managers enjoy (or dislike) cooking, some households may eat out relatively infrequently (or frequently) at both types of facility. If so, a correlation is said to exist between a household's spending at full-service restaurants and the same household's spending on fast food. Including this correlation in the model will improve its accuracy, which can be accomplished using existing procedures for simultaneously estimating models with multiple equations.[11]

Obtaining accurate estimates of the relationship between household characteristics and away-from-home expenditures requires a special statistical procedure to account for households that do not have any such expenditures. During the 2-week survey period, 21 percent of households completing the CES spent no money on fast food, and 45 percent spent no money at a full-service restaurant. This lack of purchases is known as zero-censoring, and raises some estimation problems. If the data contain many zero-expenditure observations, results based on usual methods of estimation could be biased.

Models that allow a researcher to estimate multiple equations simultaneously and to account for zero-censoring include those developed by Heien and Wessells (1990) and Shonkwiler and Yen (1999). Here, we apply the latter model because it appears to be the most accurate and is "state-of-the-art."[12] A briefdescription of this model follows, and a more detailed description is supplied in the appendix.

The Shonkwiler and Yen method proceeds in two steps to correct for the problem of zero-censoring. In our study, the first step analyzes whether each household completing the CES had non-zero expenditures in each market segment. In particular, the probability that a household spends some money on fast food is estimated as a function of the household's income, time constraints, and demographic characteristics. The same equation is also estimated for each household's decision about whether to spend some money at full-service restaurants. These results are then used in the second step. At this point, we derive equations relating a household's income and demographic characteristics to its expenditures in both market segments. These equations contain an adjustment to correct for the fact that many households spent nothing, which is based on the results of estimating the aforementioned probabilities in the first step. The adjusted equations for spending at fast food and at full-service restaurants can then be estimated using ordinary techniques for the simultaneous estimation of multiple equations.

Definition of Variables

Data in the CES must be prepared for use in the statistical model before the analysis can be conducted. In particular, variables must be calculated from the raw data in the CES. We specify and create several variables, such as measures of household expenditures, household income, hours worked by household managers, household structure, the age of a household manager, and the number of people living in a household (Table 2).

To calculate the values of per capita expenditures at fast food and full-service restaurants, we divided a household's weekly expenditures at each type of facility by the number of members in the household. Inflation-adjusted spending was then determined by dividing expenditures by the Consumer Price Index (CPI)[13] for all items.

Since income is a key variable that explains spending, we calculated this variable from data in the CES as well. To do so, we divided a household's total income by the number of household members to obtain per capita income. Per capita income was then made weekly (divided by 52) and stated in real terms (divided by the CPI).

Data in the CES were also used to calculate hours worked each week outside of the home by the household manager. However, the CES does not identify the household manager—the person primarily responsible for household chores. Yen (1993), who also used the CES, circumvented this issue by studying the impact of hours worked by married women. However, this study takes a slightly different approach. Each household's manager is defined as the survey respondent if the person was single. For married respondents, the household manager is assumed to be the spouse who works the fewest hours outside the home.[14]

Three binary variables were also created to capture household structure. Each variable corresponds to one of the three nontraditional types of household identified in this report. These variables equal "one" if the household belongs to a certain type, and "zero" otherwise. For example, one variable identifies whether a household includes only a single person. It equals one for the 28 percent of households in our sample who are single, and zero for the other 72 percent. All households were classified as belonging to either oneof the three types of nontraditional household or as being a traditional household.[15]

Table 2. Variables Measuring Expenditures and Household Characteristics, Calculated from CES

Variable	Mean	Definition
Expenditures:		
Full-service restaurant	$8.43	Per capita, average weekly spending at full-service restaurants
Fast food	$8.15	Per capita, average weekly spending on fast food
Household characteristics:		
Income	$422.00	Household's per capita, average weekly, real, before-tax income
Hours worked by manager	24.2	Hours spent in the labor force by the household manager
Age of manager	47.55	Age of the household manager
College-educated manager	0.25	Indicator variable of whether household manager has a college education
Size of household	2.56	Number of members reported to be living in the household
Race:		
Asian	0.047	Indicator variable of whether respondent or spouse identified themselves as Asian
Black	0.09	Indicator variable of whether respondent or spouse identified themselves as Black
Hispanic	0.11	Indicator variable of whether respondent or spouse identified themselves as Hispanic
Household type:		
Traditional	0.27	Indicator variable of whether respondent is married with live-at-home children
Single	0.28	Indicator variable of whether respondent lives alone
Multiple adults without children	0.35	Indicator variable of whether respondent lives with at least one other adult but no children
Single parent	0.10	Indicator variable of whether respondent is an unmarried adult with live-at-home children

Three binary variables were also created to capture household structure. Each variable corresponds to one of the three nontraditional types of household identified in this report. These variables equal "one" if the household belongs to a certain type, and "zero" otherwise. For example, one variable identifies whether a household includes only a single person. It equals one for the 28 percent of households in our sample who are single, and zero for the other 72 percent. All households were classified as belonging to either oneof the three types of nontraditional household or as being a traditional household.[15]

Other household characteristics in our model include the age of the household manager; number of people living in the household; whether the household manager had completed college or attained a higher level of education; household region; year the survey was completed; season in which the survey was completed; and whether a member of the household described himself or herself as belonging to a minority group including Black, Asian, or Hispanic.

Results of Model Estimation

The results of our statistical analysis agree with both economic theory and past studies. Household structure, a variable not considered in past studies, also is found to have a statistically significant impact on how much a household spends in each segment of the market. Estimated relationships are evaluated at the sample means shown in Table 2. The results describe how an average household could be expected to adjust its expenditures in response to a change in a variable, such as its income or household type (Table 3). Other statistical results are supplied in the appendix.

Spending in both market segments responds positively to an increase in per capita income. However, a 10-percent increase in per capita income would cause a typical household to augment its per capita expenditures on fast food by about 3.2 percent, versus 6.4 percent for full-service restaurants. Like past studies, including Byrne et al. (1998), and McCracken and Brandt (1987), our analysis suggests that households with more income buy more leisure as well as more of other dining amenities.

Time spent by the household manager in the labor force also has significant implications for how much ahousehold spends away from home. Spending for fast food is especially sensitive. A typical household increases its per capita spending on fast food by about 1.4 percent following a 10-percent increase in the number of hours worked outside the home by its manager. By contrast, this same household would increase its per person spending at full-service restaurants by only about 0.5 percent. The link between time constraints and spending for fast food—but not for full-service restaurants—has been established.

The impact of aging also varies by market segment. Households with older managers dine at fast food establishments less frequently and, as a consequence, spend less money. An increase of 10 percent in the age of a household manager reduces the same household's per capita expenditures on fast food by about 6 percent. However, the same increase in age does not negatively affect spending at full-service restaurants (Table 3). As other studies have found, people's preferences for food and services may tend to favor full-service restaurants as they age.

Larger households spend less money per capita in both market segments. This finding supports prior research arguing that economies exist in purchasing and preparing meals at home. A typical household can be expected to reduce such spending in both market segments about 2percent following a 10-percent increase in the number of people living in the household (Table 3).

Table 3. Relationship between Household Characteristics and Expected Expenditures

Characteristic	Full-service	Fast food
Change in expenditures due to a 10-percent increase in the variable:		
	Percent	
Income	+6.4	+3.2
Hours worked by manager	+0.53	+1.44
Size of household	-2.25	-1.74
Age of manager	+1.05	-5.99
Absolute change in expenditure due to household taking on the characteristic:		
	Dollars	
College-educated manager	+2.15	+0.24
Single-person household	+2.92	+2.68
Single-parent family	-0.83	-0.83
Multiple adults		
without children	+1.98	+0.89
Asian household	+0.81	+0.39
Black household	-2.87	+0.01
Hispanic household	-0.93	+0.14

Household structure also is important. However, because of the way variables capturing this structure are defined, we must be careful to interpret our results. The most appropriate interpretation of variables capturing household structure is to consider how a nontraditional household with otherwise typical characteristics would likely adjust its spending away from home if it became a traditional household. For example, as compared with a traditional household, higher per capita expenditures are typical of single-person and childless households. Indeed, a single person spends almost $3 more per person at each type of establishment. Thus, a single person could be expected to reduce his or her per capita spending away from home by $3 (for both fast food and full-service food) if he or she married and had a child.

Single parents and their children are the only type of household tending to spend less per capita than traditional households. Single parents spend about 83 cents less per person at each type of establishment than do their married counterparts. It follows that a married person with children and otherwise typical characteristics can be expected to reduce spending on fast food by 83 cents per person per week should he or she divorce or become widowed.

Other variables, like race and education, are also significant determinants of how much a household spends away from home. For instance, between 1998 and 2000, when all other variables are set at their mean value, a Black household still spent $2.87 less per person at full-service restaurants than did other households (Table 3). This finding is consistent with past studies, and may reflect differences in tastes, or possibly more limited access to foodservice establishments.

Simulating Future Away-From-Home Expenditures

Future changes in demand can be simulated by incorporating into our statistical model expectations about how key variables may change. These projected changes are based on modest growth in income, no change in hours worked by household managers, and the likely evolution of demographic variables, such as age of household managers, between 2000 and 2020. This same procedure has been used by Blaylock andSmallwood (1986), Blisard and Blaylock (1993), and Blisard et al. (2003).

One way to interpret our simulation is as a snapshot of how people would have behaved in 2000, if the projected changes in the population for 2020 were already in place in 2000. For instance, we might ask how spending on fast food would have been different in 2000 if household types assumed the same proportions as we expect in 2020. This interpretation is the best one because of a number of assumptions we have to make. First, we assume there will be no

Table 4. Current and projected future population characteristics, used in simulation

Characteristic	2000	2020
Based on BLS reports:		
Income[1]	$422.10	$514.98
Hours worked by manager[2]	24.2 hours	24.2 hours
Based on Census projections:		
Size of household	2.5 members	2.4 members
Age of manager[3]	47.33 years	49.4 years
College-educated manager	23.5% of households	26.4% of households
Single-person household	25.8% of households	28.6% of households
Single-parent household	9.2% of households	8.7% of households
Multiple adults, no children[4]	41.5% of households	46% of households
Asian household	3.9% of households	5% of households
Black household	12.3% of households	12.9% of households
Hispanic household	12.6% of households	18% of households

[1] Future income is calculated assuming a 1-percent rate of growth in per capita, real income. In particular, we used the formula for future value and continuous compounding, i.e., Income2020 = Income2000(1 + 0.01)20.

[2] No change is assumed in hours worked by household managers. Our assumption is based on the observation that measures of the working status of adult Americans, such as the female labor force rate, have been relatively stable over the past 10 years.

[3] The age of a household manager is derived from projections in Cromartie (2002). It is the average age of all people older than 19 years.

[4] Derived from Cromartie, 2002, who provides projections for traditional, single-person, and single-parent households. He also provides a projection for married couples without children. However, these four categories are not all encompassing. Some household types do not belong to any group, e.g., unmarried, cohabitating adults without children. Thus, in this study, we derived projections for households comprised of multiple adults by determining the percentage of households who could not be classified as belonging to any one of the other three groups. It follows that this fourth group includes all households with multiple adults and no children.

change in the price of fast food relative to the price of food at full-service restaurants. If such a change were to occur, it could cause households to spend more or less than the simulated amount. Second, we assume that household characteristics will continue to influence consumer behavior in the same way. For example, as a consumer moves from one demographic group to another, his or her preferences will take on the characteristics of the new group. Thus, an elderly person in 2020 is assumed to have the same expenditure patterns as an elderly person in 2000 with similar characteristics (some evidence to justify this latter assumption is provided by Blisard (2001) for the case of spending away from home). Third, our simulation holds constant factors like the number and location of restaurants as well as the mix of food and services supplied by restaurants. For instance, it is assumed that fast food restaurants will continue to supply the same types of food and the same dining amenities as they did in 2000. We will later consider the significance of relaxing this assumption, i.e., fast food restaurants offering more varied menus and heightened services.

Table 5. Simulated Change in Per Capita Spending Due to Economic and Demographic Trends

Trend	Full-service	Fast food
	Percent	
1-percent annual growth in real income	+14.86	+6.67
Increasing proportion of alternative household types	+2.17	+1.33
Aging	+0.48	-2.44
Decreasing household sizes	+0.97	+0.67
Increased levels of education	+0.72	+0.11
Racial and ethnic diversity	-0.72	+0.22
Net effect of all anticipated developments	+18	+6

Projected changes in the U.S. population include modest growth in household incomes. Real per capita disposable income increased by 1.2 percent per year on average between 1988 and 1998 (Saunders and Su, 1999). Thus, we assume that per capita incomes will rise by 1 percent per year on an inflation-adjusted basis between 2000 and 2020.[16]

No change is projected in the time constraints faced by household managers, as we have found no compelling evidence to suggest that such changes will occur. In recent years, the growth in labor force participation among adult women has slowed. The BLS reports that participation was 51.6 percent in January 1980, 57.7 percent in January 1990, and 60.3 percent in January2000. It then fell back to 59.8 percent in December 2002. We assume that, between 2000 and 2020, there will be no further changes in labor force participation, nor in how much a typical household manager works outside of the home.

The future demographic characteristics of households are derived from Cromartie (2002).[17] Population, household, and education projections used here are derived from reports by the U.S. Census Bureau. The Census Bureau population series includes projections by single year of age, sex, race, Hispanic origin, and nativity (foreign-born or native) out to the year 2100. By contrast, educational attainment projections by sex and race are available for the years 2003 and 2028, soour numbers represent interpolations between these two dates.

Projections derived from Cromartie (2002) are not intended as forecasts or predictions; rather, they represent assumptions about future trends in population, household formation, schooling, and the economy at large. For instance, in the population series, projections are based on assumptions about fertility, mortality, and immigration. In fact, differing assumptions were presented to provide three different projection series, representing high, middle, and low alternatives. This study uses projections based upon the middle series. Despite uncertainty about the extent of changes, the finding in Cromartie (2002) is that the Nation's future population will be older, better educated, live in smaller households, be racially and ethnically more diverse, and live in more nontraditional types of households (Table 4).

Future Spending at Full-Service Restaurants

The simulated net effect of all developments in the population is to lift per capita spending by about 18 percent at full-service restaurants between 2000 and 2020.[18] Rising incomes, changing household structures, and decreasing household sizes contribute significantly to this growth (Table 5). Aging and other projected developments in the population have only a small impact on spending in this market segment.[19]

Rising incomes have the greatest impact of all projected developments in the population on per capita spending at full-service restaurants. According to our simulation, if incomes rise by 1 percent annually between 2000 and 2020 and all other variables remain unchanged, spending at full-service restaurants will increase by just under 15 percent per capita by 2020. In the near future, households with more income will be buying more leisure, variety, and dining amenities.

Expected developments in household structure have the next largest impact on spending at full-service restaurants. As the proportion of households characterized as traditional decreases, spending at full-service restaurants will increase by about 2 percent per person. Though small relative to the effect of changes in income, this impact is still significant given the dollar size of this market.

Decreasing household sizes will further increase per person spending at full-service restaurants by just under 1 percent. Larger households spend less away from home (per capita) because of economies in purchasing and preparing meals and snacks at home.

Future Spending on Fast Food

The simulated net effect of all developments in the U.S. population is to lift per capita spending by about 6 percent on fast food between 2000 and 2020.[20] Rising incomes, changing household structures, decreasing household sizes, and aging will all be influential. However, unlike the other developments, the aging of the population will subdue growth in per capita spending on fast food (Table 5).

The Changing Face of Fast Food

Many fast food restaurant companies are offering an increasingly wide range of goods and services. In fact, a new kind of restaurant concept is also emerging, fast-casual, which tries to combine the convenience of fast food with the kinds of menus more typically found in a full-service restaurant. This changing face of fast food can be seen in the history of one of America's best-known restaurant chains, McDonald's.

McDonald's began as a fast food concept in 1948, when the McDonald brothers eliminated many of the menu items and dining amenities previously available at their full-service restaurant. The remaining core menu had six products - hamburgers, cheeseburgers, fries, soft drinks, coffee, and shakes. The brothers also ceased to employ waitstaff, and replaced their short-order cooks with workers who specialized at specific tasks like grilling burgers. Says the company, "this limited menu concept triggered the 'fast food' concept, because focusing on just a few items that were prepared with standardized procedures made food service a model of efficiency" (McDonald's Corporation, media website).

The menu at McDonald's has gradually expanded to again include a wider variety of menu items. The first addition to McDonald's original menu was the Filet-O-Fish™ in 1963. A handful of other now well-known products were then promoted over the next few decades including the Big Mac™ (1968), apple pie (1968), Egg McMuffin™ (1973), cookies (1974), and Chicken McNuggets™ (1983). However, according to Consortium

Members, a group representing about 350 McDonald's franchisees, more recent new product introductions have been the most "ambitious" in the company's history (Zuber, 2001).

Efforts to improve the atmosphere at McDonald's stores have accompanied efforts to expand menu items. In fact, the first McDonald's restaurant built to accommodate indoor seating was opened in 1962. However, the most noticeable efforts appear to be aimed at families with children. Ray Kroc, who became the company's franchising agent in 1954 and later purchased the McDonald's chain in 1961, is credited with focusing the company's marketing strategy on children through characters like Ronald McDonald. "A child who loves our TV commercials," Kroc is quoted as saying, "and brings her grandparents to a McDonald's gives us two more customers" (Schlosser, 2001). Notable child-oriented goods and services include packaging meals for children with toys, known as Happy Meals™ (1979), and installing play equipment in selected restaurants, known as a Playland™ (1971).

Offering more goods and services has required McDonald's to rethink how it operates. In fact, in 1998, the company replaced its much-touted kitchens with the "Made for You" production system. According to the company, "Food is prepared to order for each customer. Somebody doesn't want pickles on a Big Mac or wants mustard on a grilled chicken sandwich? No problem…What's especially exciting is that this is far more than just an operating system. It provides a platform for food innovation because it makes it easier to serve a greater variety of products" (McDonald's Corporation, 1998 Annual Report).

Many companies are promoting a newer concept, fast-casual, which strives to combine the food and atmosphere of full-service restaurants with the convenience of fast food. Examples include Boston Market, Chili's Express, and Schlotzsky's Deli. As of 2003, the McDonald's Corporation continues to own Boston Market.

Per capita spending on fast food increases with incomes. If all other variables remain unchanged and incomes increase by 1 percent annually, such spending would increase by just under 7 percent by 2020. Households with more income are likely to buy more leisure for their manager.

Changes in household structure and decreasing household sizes should lead to increased spending for fast food. The net effect of these developments is to increase per capita spending for fast food by about 2 percent. For example, as smaller households findcooking at home relatively less economical than larger ones, spending on fast food will grow.

The aging of the population will subdue any increase in spending due to changes in household structure and size. Our simulation suggests that per person spending on fast food may decrease by over 2 percent with the aging of the population. One possibility is that older people derive less satisfaction from the foods and services traditionally offered at these establishments.

IMPLICATIONS FOR MARKET COMPOSITION

Changes in demand are driving changes in the relative sizes of each segment of the away-from-home market. Rising incomes, the growing incidence of nontraditional households, and other developments in the U.S. population will allow for growth in both of the two largest market segments. However, population trends seem to favor increased spending at full-service restaurants relative to fast food.

How might restaurant companies adjust their businesses in response to the identified shift in demand? Our simulation has made some strict assumptions about prices and the behavior of consumers and firms. We now relax the assumption about firm behavior.

One plausible response by fast food companies would be to introduce more of the foods and services traditionally offered by full-service restaurants. In fact, among some companies, such a response appears to be underway. For example, many Subway restaurants accept debit and credit cards, and McDonald's has announced the same—despite reservations about its effect on the speed of its service. However, in tests using high-speed connections, McDonald's found that electronic payments can now be processed in only 5 seconds, versus 8 to 10 seconds for cash payments (*CNNMoney*, November 2002).

Many fast food restaurants are also expanding the variety of their menus. A study by the National Restaurant Association estimated that more than 75 percent of fast food restaurants introduced new menu items in 2000, while 66 percent intended to add new food items in 2001 (Operations Report 2001). At McDonald's restaurants, for example, Big Macs™ are now sold alongside newer products like breakfast bagels, salads, fruit and yogurt parfaits, and soft-service cream with candy mix-ins. In 2003, the company was further considering an increase in its scope of healthy menu items, including sliced fruits and vegetables (see box, "The Changing Face of Fast Food").

The response of fast food restaurant companies varies by firm, and the ability of many such restaurant companies to adapt may be limited. Marketing and logistics will likely prevent many fast food chains from aggressively expanding their menus and/or scope of services. First, some chains appear to worry about confusing their brand identity. Chick-fil-A, for one, added its first new category in 6 years in 2001, a portable salad line called "Cool Wraps." The vice president of brand development conceded that "We are kind of a slow poke for development because we believe in continuance of the menu" (Yee, 2001).[21] Second, fast food chains may jeopardize the speed of their service in offering too many services or menu items.

There is also the behavior of full-service restaurant companies to consider. These companies could both open more outlets and offer more variety/dining amenities at each establishment. In fact, in 2001, full-service restaurants were offering 31.6 percent more items on their menu than in 1997 (Yee, 2001). They were also increasing the scope of their services, including new options for takeout. In short, full-service restaurants may try to capture the growing demand for varied menu items among consumers who also remain time-starved.

In conclusion, the relative growth of the fast food segment appears to have stalled. Trends in demand now favor full-service dining. However, any changes in market share between the two segments will also depend on other factors, such as how firms in both market segments change the mix of foods and services supplied to their customers. Future research is needed to better understand these later changes as well as their implications for industry structure and the health of the American population.[22]

ACKNOWLEDGMENTS

The authors thank Mark Denbaly and Nicole Ballenger for their assistance in preparing this report. For review comments on earlier drafts, we also thank Oral Capps, Jr., John Park, Chung Huang, Wen Chern, and Geoffrey Paulin. Thanks too to Dale Simms for editing and production. Any remaining errors and omissions are solely the responsibility of the authors.

APPENDIX

The first step in the statistical analysis was to model whether a household purchased some food at a full-service and/or a fast food establishment. These two decisions are motivated by the following random utility model:

$$Y^*_{mh} = \gamma'_m W_h + U_{mh}$$

where Y^*_{mh} is the difference between the benefit andcost of consumption in market segment m for household h, W_h is a vector of household characteristics, $\gamma_m$is vector of parameters relating W_h to Y_{mh}, and U_{mh} isa normally distributed error term. Variables includedin W_h are the explanatory variables in Table 2, whichare thought to determine a household's likelihood ofpurchasing food away from home, as well as variablesto control for the year when the survey was administered, the season when the survey was administered, and the household's region. It is then assumed thathouseholds buy some food in market m if and only if$Y^*_{mh}>0$,i.e., the benefits exceed the costs for somenonzero level of spending. We next denote householdh's observed decision at the first stage as

$$Y_{mh} = 1 \text{ if } Y^*_{mh} > 0$$

$$Y_{mh} = 0 \text{ if } Y^*_{mh} \leq 0$$

Finally, given our assumption that U_{mh} is normallydistributed, the probability that household h makessome positive purchase in market m is represented as

$$\Pr ob(Y^*_{mh} > 0) = \Phi(\gamma'_m W_h) \quad (1)$$

where$\Phi(\gamma_m w_h)$ is the cumulative normal distributionevaluated at $\gamma_m w_h$. The statistical analysis of (1) produces the coefficient values reported in appendix Table1, as well as the reported standard errors of these estimates.

In the second step of the model of Shonkwiler and Yen(1999), we estimate a household's expenditures usingour estimates of the unknown parameters, $\hat{\gamma}_m$, from thefirst step. In particular, expenditure by the hth household in the mth market is modeled as

$$FAFH_{mh} = \Phi(\hat{\gamma}_m W_h) X'_h \beta_m + \delta_m \varphi(\gamma'_m W_h) + \varepsilon_{mh} \quad (2)$$

where$FAFH_{mh}$ is h's total expenditure in market m, $\varphi(\gamma_m W_h)$ is the normal probability distribution evaluated at $\gamma_m w_h$, x_h is a vector of household characteristics explaining expenditures, $\boldsymbol{\beta}_m$ and δ_m are a vector ofunknown parameters, and ε_{mh} is a normally distributederror term.

Appendix Table 1. Parameter Estimates and Standard Errors for Selected Variables at First Step

	Full-service	Fast food
Constant	-0.1866*	1.319*
	(0.0744)	(0.0864)
Income	0.0011*	0.0004*
	(0.0001)	(0.0001)
Income-squared	-0.0000002*	-0.00000008*
	(0.00000002)	(0.00000001)
Hours worked by manager	0.0026*	0.0064*
	(0.0007)	(0.0008)
Size of household	-0.003	0.036*
	(0.0110)	(0.0131)
Age of manager	0.0007	-0.0137*
	(0.0007)	(0.0008)
College-educated manager	0.2338*	0.1557*
	(0.0275)	(0.0327)
Single-person household	-0.3301*	-0.3827*
	(0.0437)	(0.0516)
Single-parent family	-0.2603*	-0.1924*
	(0.0423)	(0.0492)
Multiple adults without children	-0.0219	-0.0629
	(0.0329)	(0.0399)
Asian household	-0.1046*	-0.2182*
	(0.0525)	(0.0599)
Black household	-0.4926*	-0.1939*
	(0.0400)	(0.0429)
Hispanic household	-0.1979*	-0.1716*
	(0.0372)	(0.0426)
Log-likelihood	-9139.236	-6629.114
Likelihood ratio index	0.07767	0.09805

* Denotes statistical significance at the 5 percent level.

The variables in X_h also include many of the explanatory variables in Table 2, with a notable exception. Asother authors using two-step models have also done, we omit hours worked by the household manager fromX_h. "Market labor hours constrains the amount oftime available for household production and so isassumed to have a positive effect on the decision toconsume food-away-from-home," argue Byrne et al. (1996). "However, once the decision to consumefood-away-from-home is made, there is little basis tosuggest that the number of hours worked would affectthe expenditure level."

Maximum likelihood estimates of the unknown parameters are reported in appendix Table 2. The standarderrors of these coefficient estimates have been calculated using the method of Murphy and Topel (1985)and are also reported in the table.

Appendix Table 2. Estimated Coefficients and Standard Errors for Selected Variables at Second Step

	Full-service	Fast food
$\Phi(\gamma'_m W_h)$	10.90	13.07
	(6.764)	(0.8989)
$\Phi(\gamma'_m W_h)$ X Income	0.0118*	0.0056*
	(0.0056)	(0.0011)
$\Phi(\gamma'_m W_h)$ X Income-squared	-0.0000007	-0.0000012*
	(0.0000015)	(0.0000002)
$\Phi(\gamma'_m W_h)$ X Size of household	-1.293*	-1.024*
	(0.3017)	(0.1294)
$\Phi(\gamma'_m W_h)$ X Age of manager	0.0247	0.0013
	(0.0206)	(0.0211)
$\Phi(\gamma'_m W_h)$ X College-educated manager	0.8359	-1.107*
	(1.173)	(0.3786)
$\Phi(\gamma'_m W_h)$ X Single-person household	9.874*	7.201*
	(1.819)	(0.6376)
$\Phi(\gamma'_m W_h)$ X Single-parent family	1.152	0.6045
	(1.646)	(0.4780)
$\Phi(\gamma'_m W_h)$ X Multiple adults w/o children	3.519*	1.574*
	(0.8206)	(0.3776)
$\Phi(\gamma'_m W_h)$ X Asian household	2.975*	2.776*
	(1.474)	(0.7031)
$\Phi(\gamma'_m W_h)$ X Black household	1.078	1.959*
	(2.785)	(0.5841)
$\Phi(\gamma'_m W_h)$ X Hispanic household	0.9039	1.911*
	(1.466)	(0.4975)
$\Phi(\gamma'_m W_h)$	-4.120	-14.40*
	(7.696)	(3.5200)
System-weighted R^2	0.3453	

*Denotes statistical significance at the 5-percent level.

References

Becker, G. (1965). "A Theory of the Allocation of Time," *Economic Journal,75*, 493-517.

Blaylock, J.& D. Smallwood. (1986). *U.S. Demand for Food: Household Expenditures, Demographics, and Projections*, U.S. Department of Agriculture, Economic Research Service, TB-1713.

Blisard, N.& J. Blaylock. (1993).*U.S. Demand for Food: Household Expenditures, Demographics, and Projections for 1990-2010*, U.S. Department of Agriculture, Economic Research Service, TB-1818.

Blisard, N. (2001). *Income and Food ExpendituresDecomposed by Cohort, Age, and Time Effects,* U.S. Department of Agriculture, Economic Research Service, TB-1896.

Blisard, N., Variyam, J. & Cromartie, J. (2003). *Food Expenditures by U.S. Households: Looking Ahead to 2020*, U.S. Department of Agriculture, Economic Research Service, AER-821.

Byrne, P., Capps, Jr.O. & Saha, A. (1996). "Analysis of Food-Away-from-Home Expenditure Patterns for U.S. Households, 1982-89," *American Journal of Agricultural Economics* ,78, 614-627.

Byrne, P., Capps Jr. O. & Saha, A. (1998) "Analysis of Quick-serve, Mid-scale, and Up-scale Food Away from Home Expenditures," *The International Food and Agribusiness Management Review ,1*, 51-72.

CNNMoney. "McDonald's to accept plastic," 11/26/2002. [Online]: www.cnn.com.

Consumer Expenditure Survey. Bureau of Labor Statistics. 1998, 1999, and 2000.

Cromartie, J. (2002) "Population Growth and Demographic Change, 1980-2020," *FoodReview,25, 1*, 10-12.

Food CPI, Prices & Expenditures: Expenditure Tables. Economic Research Service. 04/30/03 [Online]: www.ers.usda.gov/briefing/CPIFoodAnd Expenditures.*Foodservice 2010*. McKinsey & Company, 2001.

Friddle, C., Mangaraj, S. & Kinsey, J. (2001) "The Food Service Industry: Trends and Changing Structure in the New Millenium,"Working Paper #01-02, The Retail Food Industry Center, University of Minnesota.

Gogoi, P.& M. Arndt."Hamburger Hell," *Business Week*, 3/3/2003, pp. 104-108.

Green, H. (1964). *Aggregation in Economic Analysis*, Princeton University Press.

Heien, D.&Wessells.C. (1990). "Demand Systems Estimation with Microdata:A Censored Regression Approach, " *Journal of Business and Economic Statistics* , *8*, 365-71.

Hiemstra, S.& Kim.W.G. (1995). "Factors Affecting Expenditures for Food Away From Home in Commercial Establishment by Type of Eating Place and Meal Occasion, " *Hospitality Research Journal, 19*, 15-31.

Jekanowski, M., Binkley, J. & Eales, J. (2001). "Convenience, Accessibility, and the Demand for Fast Food," *Journal of Agricultural and Resource Economics, 26*, 58-74.

Kinsey, J. (1990). "A graphic look at key economic figures. Diverse demographics drive the food industry," *Choices, 5*, 22-23.

Lin, B. & Frazao, E. (1999). *Away-From-Home Foods Increasingly Important to Quality of American Diet*, U.S. Department of Agriculture, Economic Research Service, AIB-749.

Manchester, A. (1987). *Developing an Integrated Information System for the Food Sector*, U.S. Department of Agriculture, Economic Research Service, AER-575.

McCracken, V., & Brandt, J. (1987). "Household Consumption of Food Away from Home: Total Expenditure and by Type of Food Facility," A*merican Journal of Agricultural Economics, 69*, 274-84.

Murphy, K. & Topel, R. (1985). "Estimation and Inference in Two-step Econometric Models," *Journal of Business and Economic Statistics, 3*, 370-379.

Nayga, Jr., R. M. & Capps, Jr. O. (1994). "Impact of SocioEconomic and Demographic Factors on Food Away from Home Consumption: Number of Meals and by Type of Facility," *Journal of Restaurant and Foodservice Marketing, 1*, 45-69.

Operations Report 2001, National Restaurant Association, Washington, DC, 2001.

Restaurant Industry 2010: The Road Ahead, National Restaurant Association, Washington, DC, 1999.

Restaurant Industry Forecast 2003, National Restaurant Association, Washington, DC, 2003.

Saunders, N. & Su, B. (1999). "The U.S. Economy to 2008: A Decade of Continued Growth," *Monthly Labor Review*. U.S. Dept. Commerce, Bureau of Labor Statistics, Nov.

Schlosser, E. (2001). *Fast Food Nation*. New York: Houghton Mifflin Company.

Shonkwiler, J. S.& Yen, S. (1999). "Two-Step Estimation of a Censored System of Equations." *American Journal of Agricultural Economics, 81*, 972-982.

Smallwood, D. & Blaylock, J. (1981). *Impact of Household Size and Income on Food Spending Patterns*, United States Department of Agriculture, Economic Research Service, TB-1650.

Su, S. & Yen, S. (2000). "A Censored System of Cigarette and Alcohol Consumption," *Applied Economics, 32*, 729-37.

Yee, L. "Bold New Day," *Restaurants and Institutions*, 07/15/2001, pp. 24-32.

Yen, S. (1993). "Working Wives and Food away from Home: The Box-Cox Double Hurdle Model," *American Journal of Agricultural Economics, 75*, 884-95.

Yen, S., Kan, K. & Su, S. (2002). "Household Demand for Fats and Oils" Two-Step Estimation of a Censored Demand System," *Applied Economics, 34*, 1799-1806.

Zuber, A. "McD president says chain will emphasize food, not trim menu offerings," *Nation's Restaurant News*, 04/16/2001, p. 1.

End Notes

[1] Figures reported in this study are supplied by the Economic Research Service (ERS) and do not include alcohol. However, estimates of total expenditures do include the value of food consumed away from home, even if not purchased, such as the value of food distributed in some institutional facilities, as well as taxes and tips. See Manchester (1987) for a more detailed explanation of how ERS figures are calculated, including the distinction between sales and expenditures. Other sources report similar estimates of the market's size even though these sources base their calculations on very different formulas. The National Restaurant Association, for one, emphasizes the value of sales by restaurant companies. For 2002, it estimated the value of sales at $407.8 billion.

[2] Industry studies have also projected the continued growth of the market including analyses by the National Restaurant Association (*Restaurant Industry 2010: The Road Ahead*) and a consulting firm (*Foodservice 2010*).

[3] The National Restaurant Association estimates that, in 2002, sales by full-service restaurants totaled $146 billion and sales by fast food restaurants amounted to $116 billion (*Restaurant Industry Forecast 2003*).

[4] Making a meal convenient includes building outlets near where consumers live, work, and shop. Convenience also means speedy service. For example, when it comes to drive-thru service, it appears that a goal among fast food chains is to serve customers in under 3 minutes. In 2002, the average service time—from when a car reaches the speaker to the car's driver receiving his or her food—at 25 major chains was about 187 seconds (Tutor, 2003).

[5] *Foodservice 2010*, a report by a consulting company, McKinsey & Co., also expresses this same view.

[6] Eating occasion was defined to include, for example, breakfast, lunch, and dinner.

[7] The National Panel Diary Group (NPD) also undertakes such a survey, Consumer Reports on Eating Share Trends (CREST). However, these data have not been available for use by outside researchers in recent years.

[8] It includes only noninstitutional households. An institutional household would include people living in institutions, such as prisons or military facilities.

[9] We also removed households providing incomplete information on key characteristics and/or reporting negative incomes from the sample. The CES designates households as "complete" or "incomplete" income reporters, depending on their response to income questions. The distinction between complete and incomplete reporters is based, in general, on whether or not the respondent provided values for major sources of income, such as wages and salaries, self-employment income, and Social Security income. However, even complete income reporters may not have provided a full accounting of all income from all sources. It is also possible for complete reporters to report negative incomes due to self-employment or other income losses. In this study, incomplete income reporters and complete reporters with negative incomes are excluded. In each year, the final sample includes about 5, 000 households.

[10] Our data were collected over 3 years. We allow prices to vary from year to year. We also allow prices to depend upon the season of the year when the survey was administered as well as upon the region of the country in which the household resides. Households are assumed to face similar prices otherwise. Studies of the away-from-home market commonly make this same assumption, including McCracken and Brandt (1987) and Byrne et al. (1998).

[11] This procedure is known as a seemingly unrelated regression.

[12] The method of Heien and Wessells (1990) has been widely applied over the past decade, including by Byrne et al. (1998). However, Shonkwiler and Yen (1999) have found a shortcoming of this model and present an alternative specification. Furthermore, they use Monte Carlo techniques to demonstrate that their proposed specification is statistically more accurate. The method of Shonkwiler and Yen (1999) has been recently applied in several studies (e.g., Su and Yen, 2000; Yen et al., 2002).

[13] Fourth quarter of 2000 = 100.

[14] This approach is straightforward for households with either only one adult or a married couple. However, it may be less clear when applied to households with multiple unmarried adults, e.g., same-sex couples. In such a case, the household manager is always the survey respondent. There are two reasons for this default approach. First, the CES does not include information on adults in a household who are not married to the survey respondent. Second, it is arguable that the action of responding to the CES is itself a domestic chore. If so, it is further likely that the person who maintains the diary section of the CES is the primary household manager.

[15] For this reason, we did not include a variable to account for whether a household was traditional. Since each household in the data is classified as belonging to one type and only one type, a proper statistical analysis requires that we omit one category of household from the analysis. This omission creates the orthogonal relationship among predictor variables that is required for estimating a covariance matrix and conducting hypothesis tests. The consequence is that the identified relationships between the three variables in the model and expenditures must be interpreted as a measure of the difference in per capita weekly spending by these households and traditional households.

[16] This same assumption was made in Blisard et al. (2003).

[17] Further information on how the projections in Cromartie (2002) are calculated can be found in Blisard et al. (2003).

[18] Simulated growth is in real terms, i.e, inflation-adjusted dollars (base = fourth quarter of 2000). Moreover, this simulation is for per capita spending. It does not reflect likely growth in total spending at full-service restaurants. This result is simulated by further considering the impact of increased growth in the size of the population. In total, assuming the population

will expand from 281 million to 332 million people (Cromartie, 2002), expenditures at full-service restaurants could rise by 40 percent.

[19] Some of these other variables may very important determinants of demand. However, between 2000 and 2020, they are not expected to change in ways that significantly alters expenditures away from home. For example, as shown in Table 2, Black households spend much less at full-service restaurants than non-Black households.

[20] Once again, simulated growth is in real terms, i.e, inflation-adjusted dollars (base = fourth quarter of 2000). Moreover, this simulation is for per capita spending. Total growth in the market is simulated by considering the projected growth in the size of the population from 281 million to 332 million people. According to our simulation, the total spending by all households on fast food will grow by 26 percent.

[21] This survey did not include fine dining establishments (i.e., restaurants with white tablecloths and a maitre'd).

[22] ERS is currently undertaking a study of restaurants to determine how they are adapting their menus and services. Evidence on this subject admittedly is anecdotal at this point in time.

INDEX

A

B

C

D

I

K

L

M

N

O

P

V

W